The Sanctuary Called Home

NANA KHIZANISHVILI

authorHOUSE®

AuthorHouse™
1663 Liberty Drive
Bloomington, IN 47403
www.authorhouse.com
Phone: 1 (800) 839-8640

Published by AuthorHouse   10/07/2019

ISBN: 978-1-7283-2983-3 (sc)
ISBN: 978-1-7283-2982-6 (e)

Library of Congress Control Number: 2019915422

Print information available on the last page.

This book is printed on acid-free paper.

Author's Photo Credit: Rachel E.H. Photography

Contents

.

Preface

There is no there there.
—Gertrude Stein

In hopes that I will bring away with me a snowflake from days gone by.
—Georges Brassens

This is not a work of fiction. This is documentary prose depicting scenes from my childhood in Georgia, a beautiful country in the Caucasus region between the Black Sea and the Caspian Sea. Some scenes stand out vividly, while some fade in the background but maintain worth and importance. All the memories are full of people and places.

My elders are gone now. The places I remember are either decayed or destroyed and redesigned. It was this disappearance that urged me to sit and write what I had committed to memory.

My family has grown and expanded since we left Georgia and made America our second home. My daughters, Tika and Annie, have started families of their own, and I felt an urgency to write about their ancestors. I owe it to my mom and dad not to sever the ties that hold us to our roots.

This book is a token of love, a tangible thread that unwinds and ends at the beginning of a road taken by my parents and their parents before them. The road is bumpy and full of surprises, but I am eager to take my grandkids—Sylvia, Louisa, and John—with me and guide them into the world kept intact in my heart. It is my heart that has selectively kept the good, kind, and dear memories and glossed over the bad and unpleasant.

Acknowledgments

My most heartfelt thanks go to my daughters, Tika and Annie, my first editors and strict critics. I sometimes managed to win an argument about bypassing grammar rules in order to preserve my style and voice. The questions they asked helped shape some of the passages to make them more comprehensible for readers who otherwise might not understand some bizarre Soviet realities.

Many thanks go to Crestmont Book Club and all my book club friends who always listened with interest to my stories and marveled at our endurance.

I am ever so grateful to my friends from those faraway days who were in my thoughts while I was writing about our shared childhood.

Gogi and Revaz, without you, my life would lack fun, mischief, competition, and adventure.

To my husband, Irakli, my loyal sounding board, and Gabo, who snoozed at my feet impatiently waiting for his evening promenade.

One

PARK STELLA

Once upon a time, I knew a magical place called Stella. It was the park of my happy childhood. I don't know where the name came from or why it was called so. I only know that the park was a constant in my childhood.

We lived in downtown Tbilisi in a beautiful neighborhood of old houses and crooked streets. Ours was an apartment in a five-story building, right across from the beautiful park called Stella. The park reigns over the most vivid recollections from the happy days of my childhood.

It had red alleyways covered with crushed red brick powder, tall cedar and pine trees, green garden benches, a restaurant in the back, and a big open stage where an orchestra played in the summer evenings. The park also had a summer movie theater, and the building was partially open. One side of it was an open balcony with pillars that held folded tarpaulins wrapped around them, to be unfolded if the evenings were rainy or windy.

Since we usually had our bedroom windows open on summer nights, I remember sounds of music and voices carried across the street in the dark of the night, often when I was already in bed. I couldn't make out all of the dialogue, as it came out muffled and slightly distorted. But I learned early on that music in movies always carried special meaning. It could be mellow and sweet or accelerated and intense. I tried to imagine what would match that music. So often I fell asleep as a princess or a detective—sometimes even an adventurer.

The end of the school year opened the summer season in the park for us, as we had more time to play. Kids gathered there from all over the neighborhood. Their ages varied, and they came from all the different backgrounds and nationalities that lived in the neighborhood at that time, including Armenians, Kurds, Russians, and Ukrainians. Everybody was united by a feeling of community and cheerful spirit.

"See you in Stella" was a happy commitment for fun and games. We played hopscotch and all kinds of ball games. We held championships in jumping rope where we competed in who could skip the longest. Everybody loved to play hide and seek, capture the flag, and blind man's bluff. We had our own counting-out rhymes to determine who would become It and stay to seek or to chase us.

Some of the rhymes were tricky. If we wanted to cheat somebody into becoming It, we would split the last word into more syllables so that the person we wanted to count out was safely out. Who stayed and became It was determined to our liking. This special treatment was usually reserved for new kids before they were finally initiated.

"One, two, three, four, five, six, seven, eight, nine, ten, eleven, you are not clever or cle-ver." The last word was uttered as a one-syllable word or divided into multiple syllables at will. The one who counted would point at an unsuspecting newcomer and complete the rhyme, thus selecting It. That unfortunate player was to stay behind at the bench or a tree, depending on what was chosen as the base, and with closed eyes count out loud until ten to give everyone else time to scatter as far as we could go and find a good hiding place.

Hiding farther away was always better. There were so many places to hide, but going outside the park limits was forbidden. Climbing a tree and hiding there was not allowed either. Some of our friends were good at quickly finding hidden playmates and tagging them back to the seeker's base. For those who were quickly found, all was not lost if they could beat It to tag the base before It did so. I remember the glee of racing to the base to tag in and be counted safe.

Some seekers would not go too far from the base so that they could quickly claim their discovery—"I see you! Come out!"—and immediately tag the base. It went without saying that seekers couldn't peep, and naturally nobody was supposed to reveal where we went. If seekers were too late, they had to close their eyes and start over.

My favorite game was called wish a soul. We would divide into two teams. Then each team would form a line, link hands, and stand at a distance from the other team's line. After lining up and positioning ourselves at a considerable distance, one of the teams would call out, "Whose soul do you wish?"

The other team would call out the name of a desired soul. The selected soul would run forward into the rival team's line of firmly held hands, aiming to break in. I remember deciding on my way which would be the weakest link to break and running toward that couple of hands.

If we could break through, we would then grab one of their teammates over to our side. If it so happened that the soul could not break the link, then that soul had to stay behind and join the rival team. It was lots of fun to race and compete. Some souls were more popular and favorable than others, so they shuttled between the two lines more often.

Capture the flag or two flags was another fun game where loyalties and sympathies were tested. You had to be fast, agile, alert, and canny. It really helped if you were a fast runner and could make quick decisions.

This was the noisiest game, with many of us running around trying to capture the enemy flag and defend our own. These games were usually accompanied by screamed commands like "Don't let them grab our flag!" or "Watch out! Watch out!" There was much running, jumping, snatching the flag, and racing to the base.

One day, somebody brought a badminton set to Stella. My elder brother, Gogi, ran home to bring our set as well. That summer, we started a badminton championship. That gave rise to lots of arguing as to who scored and who didn't. Sometimes a kid who was not that keen on playing the game acted as an umpire, trying hard to be fair and friendly. The umpire had to keep score and deal with arguing players.

"Did you see where it went?"

"But that's beyond the line!"

"Come, I'll show you!"

"Don't move. I am coming over!"

Shuttlecocks often ended up in the tall cedar trees, and we had to toss pebbles or sticks to get them down. Sometimes if we were desperate enough, somebody would throw a racket to get the shuttlecock down, but then the racket might stay lodged in the branches. Pebbles served the purpose better.

Once one of these pebbles hit a street lamp that happened to be in the way and smashed it. Oh, we were horrified! There were no grown-ups around, and nobody witnessed the disaster. Everybody ran home and didn't show up until the following day. We even stopped playing badminton for a while.

Miraculously, nobody found out what had happened. The lamp was soon replaced with no questions asked. It was such a relief. We tried not to stare at the lamp, but we were curious to find out how they replaced it. In the end, we just ignored it … and decided not to use pebbles to rescue our shuttlecocks.

There was a mulberry tree in the park. Ripe mulberries usually ended up on the treetop ready to be picked. We could shake the tree, but the mulberries would drop on the ground, and nobody wanted to pick them up off the ground and wash them. Eating off the tree had a bonus: it's how I learned to climb trees. I could climb very high, sit on a branch, and eat mulberries, not minding that they too should have been washed.

There was a big open-air stage at the end of the main alleyway partially covered by a shell-shaped roof. I remember holiday concerts but also us fooling around pretending to be famous singers and dancers.

There were some small buildings at one of the sections of the park. One of the buildings, with lots of windows and a green door, held much of our interest. The plaque on the building read "Wig Workroom." The windows were open in the summer, and we could see several workmen sitting inside at worktables, making wigs. Sometimes one of them would bring out the wigs and put them in the sun to dry. The workroom had some theater association, as the plaque also mentioned "Theater Society." For us, all of this was mysterious and fascinating.

The park also had a very friendly gardener, an old Azeri gentleman who tended to the roses and other flowers. When my younger brother, Revaz, was born, we would often take him to the park to be in the fresh air. The old gardener took a liking to him and always rewarded him with a rose. One of the first actions Revaz learned was to sniff a rose and smile with appreciation. That started his love of roses and a lifelong interest in gardening.

We could play in Stella for hours, rushing home for lunch and rushing back to pick up where we left off. When Mom came home from work, we had to go home for dinner and stay there. By then, we were ready to read books and be with the family. This happy period usually lasted for a couple of weeks, until my parents could take us on summer vacations to the mountains or the seaside or our country house—out of the hot and noisy city.

I was already in high school when one day we heard that the city council had decided to close the park for renovations. They were going to construct a building for the Georgia Theater Society there. As we understood it, the theater society building would take up a major part of the park. The main area to be affected was the old movie theater and the evergreen cedar trees in front of it. The cedar trees were tall, beautiful, and like old playmates to us, as they had trapped so many of our shuttlecocks and rackets.

The city council's decision was unfair not only because the construction would change and mutilate the park but also because the park was the only green space providing a playground and a beautiful area for rest, relaxation, and entertainment for surrounding streets, stretching along several blocks. There was no other park anywhere close by. But the city council wasted no time in pursuing its plans.

The first to go were the cedar trees. They were sawed down immediately after the decision was made. Once-gorgeous trees lay lifeless along the alleyway. It was indeed a sad sight and one that stayed with me forever.

One of our neighbors who worked at a local newspaper brought a photographer to snap photos of the damaged nature. My mom and dad wrote a letter to the Tbilisi City Council and Architectural Committee asking them to review the decision and not destroy the park. My brother Gogi and I were tasked with taking the letter to our neighbors, our friends from the park, and any acquaintances we knew in the neighborhood to secure as many signatures as possible.

We ran to our friends who lived in the area. All the neighbors signed it. The letter was compelling. All the arguments were well-grounded and convincing, and there were signatures aplenty. Then we had to wait for the reply.

It came several days later and was addressed to my dad. For some reason, it was written in Russian, and it was very succinct. Among other formal phrases, one crucial line stood out: "The park is not being destroyed but undergoes recreational development."

Other trees that were in the way of the construction were chopped down as well. The red crushed-brick cover was replaced by asphalt. Years later, when the theater society was housed in the big grey building, the remainder of the space was taken up by a parking lot. Only one or two benches were left behind as a painful reminder of the once thriving park.

Once in a while, I could see someone from the neighborhood dropping by with their kids for a bit of rest but leaving quickly because of the exhaust fumes and car noise. The sunny green park of my happy childhood was gone forever.

Two

MY STREET

The house where I lived was on a beautiful street shaded by acacia trees. The middle of the road was covered with big gray cobblestones that preserved the authenticity of the past. Our section of the street was just a block of four or five houses with big backyards.

The street looked especially beautiful in the spring when all the trees were covered with tiny green buds and the multitude of them created spheres of magical haze right before the leaves were fully unfurled. The trees later bloomed into white acacia clusters that hung from brunches emanating a sweet fragrance—the nostalgic fragrance of my childhood, sweet and tender. Most of the trees on both sides of the street were acacia trees, but there were some sycamore trees as well.

Around springtime, street vendors would appear at the corner of the street. These were peasants from nearby villages bringing their garden flowers to sell to the city dwellers. There were gorgeous lilacs with many shades of purple, magenta, and white, as well as bunches of violets, daffodils, cyclamen, and lilies of the valley. The appearance of street vendors was a sure sign that spring was setting in.

Mom's birthday was in March. She loved cyclamens and violets. These were the flowers we gave her on that day. Lilies of the valley, also her favorites, came at the end of April. The tiny tender bells on green stems had such a fragrance and carried themselves so gracefully, it is no surprise that they were best loved. There was a very beautiful navy-blue vase on the mantelpiece in Dad's study. It was my parents' wedding present and was solely used to hold lilies of the valley.

Lilacs were special flowers not only because they were one of my favorites and smelled divine but also because they could make wishes come true. The secret lay in finding the right lilac flower. Lilacs as a rule have four petals, but flowers with five petals are not unheard of, although they are rare. The idea was to look for flowers with five petals. It was time-consuming but worth it. In our childish belief, the uniqueness of five petals or occasionally six petals made them exceptional. That is why it was believed that finding them was a prediction of auspicious events and wishes coming true.

I spent minutes on end staring at bunches of lilacs looking for those promising flowers. However, just finding them was not enough. You had to make a wish and then eat the flower. It goes without saying that we were on a special lilac diet in the spring.

Much as the street was beautiful in the spring, it was equally stunning in the winter months when it snowed. It didn't snow often in Tbilisi; only if winters were especially cold. It could snow for several days but never longer than two or three weeks. The snow itself did not last long until it turned into a muddy slush.

The first snow brought out a quiet, dignified silence in the evenings. It softened the bustling city noise and slowed down activities. I loved those nights when our street was all dressed in white and there were not many cars out to mar the white road.

The street sloped a little, and some kids even managed to go sledding. However, the slope was not steep enough for a real joyride. Snow in Tbilisi was also the time to get hit by snowballs. Snowball fights were really popular.

I loved watching the snowfall. If you watch falling snow for a long time, you start noticing that snowflakes do not really fall to the ground but rather float up. I remember I observed this optical illusion when I once stayed at home sick in bed and watched the falling snow from my bedroom window. I was so fascinated that I got up to see if anything was sticking to the ground. I wondered how that was even possible, one way or the other.

Our house was a five-story apartment building with two entrances. All the houses back then had centralized heating systems and a strict schedule for turning on the heat—not earlier than the first week in November. Since fall was usually mild, we kept the windows and the balcony door open to let the fresh air in until it really got chilly. As the house was almost at the foot of a mountain, the air was crisp and refreshing. The building had a big backyard where some of the residents had their garages and sheds. There were poplar trees in the yard and a nice play area for kids.

Our yard could be full of activity. In the early days of my childhood, seeing vagrants visiting backyards was quite common. These people were sometimes quite enterprising and offered entertainment. Some were so talented, they would even sing arias from operas. Children helped them collect the money if the neighbors tossed down "concert fees" from upstairs windows.

Occasionally, an old ragman with a big sack slung over his back would appear calling out, "Collecting old clothes! Used clothes, old clothes!" We had clothes set aside for our share of the contribution. He always left with his sack full of old garb which we gladly donated.

Another frequent visitor was a knife grinder, calling out, "Knives and scissors to grind!" He carried a small machine tool with whetstones that he operated with a foot pedal. It was fun to watch him at work and see the sparks fly. He sometimes told us to stand back, and we complied, as we feared we would catch on fire.

It was a common sight to see milk and yogurt sellers arriving from nearby villages early in the mornings. They would collect empty milk bottles and yogurt jars from their regular customers and leave fresh dairy products. These vendors would also have greens and vegetables from their vegetable gardens, depending on the season. Sometimes street vendors would also sell potatoes, cherries, tomatoes, cranberries, and other produce.

It could also happen that several of them would come into the yard at the same time, and competing offers would be heard in the neighborhood:

"Pears!"

"Fresh tomatoes!"

"Sour cherries!"

"Ice cream! Ice cream!"

It was a special high-pitched singsong calling out in both Georgian and Russian. We would run downstairs to get ice cream. Some neighbors from upstairs would lower their baskets on ropes with money inside and lift the groceries or ice cream up to their floor.

Then there was a vendor selling popcorn that was dyed pink. A fistful of popcorn was assembled into balls. *Bati-buti* is a Georgian word for popcorn. When a *bati-buti* vendor came into our yard, my brother Gogi and I were strictly prohibited from ever buying the popcorn, as my mom was convinced that the *bati-buti* was created in unsanitary conditions. It was true that the bag the balls were kept in was always gray and unappealing.

When the neighborhood kids bought *bati-buti*, we made an effort not to stare. Occasionally, one of them would take pity on us and offer us a morsel to try. We would look up at our windows to check whether anybody was watching before gobbling it up.

We seldom played in the yard, probably because we were busy during the school year. Sometimes we would play ball games or go to an ice cream café two blocks down the road. Theirs was the tastiest ice cream ever. They would serve ice cream in metallic bowls.

When we were little and Mom took us to the café, she brought demitasse spoons with her so that we could eat ice cream using our tiny spoons from home. They were silver spoons and had the most beautiful handles made of filigree design. I loved those spoons. They always made our outing to the café a special one.

For those who didn't want to go inside, a saleslady sold ice cream cones outside the café. If we were in a hurry, we would grab ice cream cones. Once, a bunch of us went to buy ice cream from her. We must have been in middle school then. We were in acting mode and pretending that we were foreign students visiting the city.

Naturally, we claimed that we didn't speak Georgian or Russian, only English. We assumed the saleslady, being Russian herself, didn't speak English. We showed with our fingers how many cones we wanted and gave her the money. She admonished us in her usual stern way not to drop the wrapping paper on the ground, as somebody had already dropped a paper near her feet. We had not even opened our cones, and what's more, we were not supposed to understand what she was saying.

Assuming a leader role, I asked her in English "What?" instead of "Pardon?" or "Excuse me?" To her ears, it sounded like the familiar Russian *vot*, meaning "here." Naturally, she thought I was agreeing with her.

She looked at me, then at the littered pavement, and continued in the same reproving tone, "I see that it's here! I am telling you not to do the same!" Obviously, we were right that she did not speak English. And I decided in the future not to show off in front of unsuspecting ice cream sellers.

There was another ice cream café farther from our house. It was in an area called Zemel. We loved going there because it was Mom's favorite place, and their ice cream was also very tasty.

Revaz loved ice cream. He loved it more than any other dessert and was ready to eat it at all times. One day when Mom was at a genetics conference in Kiev, Dad told us he would take us to the ice cream café in the evening. While we were still upstairs, Revaz ran ahead to reach the garage first and jump into the car while Dad walked downstairs.

In the middle of his run, he twisted his ankle and fell on his arm. He shouted out in pain, as any six-year-old would. Dad looked at his arm, immediately put him into the car, and rushed him to the hospital instead of the ice cream café. It was Dad himself who put the plaster on Revaz's broken arm.

When Mom returned home later that week, Revaz proudly showed her his plastered arm.

"I can't leave you alone," Mom said, upset but happy that it was just the arm and nothing more serious.

Both cafés are long gone. There is a Marriott hotel on the very spot where my childhood café stood at the corner of my street.

I knew all my neighbors, and they knew me. Some of the elderly neighbors were more talkative than others, and I tried to avoid bumping into any of them if I was in a hurry. Our neighbors from across the stairwell were originally from Poland. Aunt Yulia, as we called her in the Georgian way of addressing elder ladies, had snow-white hair and a soft voice. I don't remember how her family ended up in Georgia. I only know that her father had a bakery in the town of Kutaisi before the October Revolution.

Their recipe notebook contained amazing secrets of baking. I have never again tasted such cookies, pancakes, and cakes that melted in my mouth. I regret that we never asked for the recipes, or that I never asked Aunt Yulia to teach me to bake.

Often when Revaz returned from school and there was nobody in our apartment, he stayed with Aunt Yulia. They enjoyed each other's company. Both welcomed the opportunity to foster friendship and exchange daily news. Aunt Yulia always kept newspaper clippings that she thought would interest my brother, and naturally, she always had something yummy ready for him.

There were two ways to enter our building: from the yard and from the street, which was also the main entrance. You had to go out of the yard into the street and walk up to the main entrance from the side of the street. It was a longer route to enter the building. Dad liked to take the longer route and slowly walk to the main entrance after he returned from work and parked his car in the garage.

One evening, Dad came home from work and parked the car in the garage as usual. Also as usual, he slowly walked toward the house. That's when he noticed that the trunk of the little sycamore sapling in front of our house had been badly damaged and was drooping to the ground. Obviously, it had been hit by a car. To my dad's eyes, this was a little helpless patient in need of a surgeon's help, and he was there to provide prompt and effective treatment.

Dad called us to bring him some bandages from the apartment.

What he had in mind was to first dress the broken body of the sapling. He wrapped bandages around its trunk, then fixed the trunk to the plank that one of the neighbors had brought over and hammered firmly into the ground next to the tree. The plank was a much-needed support for the damaged sapling. We stood and watched and tried to help by holding the tree so that it did not droop over but was firmly affixed to its support. When all was finished, we watered the tree and left for the night.

The tree became our special project for a while. We were grateful to be in charge and happy to follow its revival and gradual improvement. Then when the days and months went by, the sapling turned into a beautiful tall tree, outgrowing the helpful plank. With time, the once-white bandages got dirty and tore apart, but the memories of that day never left me. I will always remember how my dad fussed around the tree and brought it back to life.

In the summer, when we left for vacation, I did not think about our street—or Tbilisi for that matter—as I looked forward to new adventures in the country. However, toward the end of the summer, I was ready to go back. I missed my home and friends. We were all so ready to show off our summer tans and exchange stories.

When I was growing up, Tbilisi was much smaller, with fewer people and fewer cars in its streets. During summer vacations, with so many families out of town, streets became less noisy. Our street was not an exception. We would return at the end of August, usually the 29th or 30th, to get ready for school and buy uniforms and school supplies. That was an unforgettable ride back, with the feeling of joy at homecoming.

On entering Tbilisi, I always had butterflies in my stomach. At that time, I did not know what nostalgia felt like. The longing for familiar surroundings, the joy of reconnecting with friends and places, and the sense of belonging were the sweetest of feelings. The street waited for us. The street missed us too. It looked almost bored in its tranquility. That peacefulness is what I miss now when I remember those faraway days at the end of the summers.

The street of my childhood home as well as other streets in the downtown started changing with time. Many buildings became dilapidated and required urgent repairs. Some really needed sprucing up, but more often than not their looks were changed as a result of incompetent architectural choices, the whims of ignorant decision-makers, and a complete disregard for the city's history and culture. The authentic look and feel of the downtown as I remember it is preserved only in my memory. It seems more precious now and intensifies the sense of nostalgia for home.

Three

SHOPPING

Sometimes when Mom went shopping, she would take us with her. I loved accompanying her to some of the stores, as they held a special interest for me. One such place was a big grocery store.

The grocery store where we went shopping was two blocks down the street. It was a uniquely beautiful place inside. It had a grandeur more appropriate to a palace than a regular grocery store. It was the only store of its kind in the whole city, and being downtown, it attracted many visitors. There were huge mirrors on the walls, marble countertops, and enormous porcelain vases in corners of the vast hall and in the shop windows.

To a child's eye, the store looked beautifully decorated inside, and I wanted to look and point out when something looked especially appealing. Mom always told us not to point with our finger, so I never did. There were canned condensed milk jars stacked in pyramids, packages of various cookies piled in different geometric shapes, and mounds of candy in vases. The place smelled of coffee and chocolate.

The store consisted of several separate departments. Salespeople were mainly ladies with starched head covers and white aprons. They stood behind the counters, and you had to go up to the counter to place your order. I loved watching them weighing butter, cheese, and sausages. Then they would take a large piece of thick brown paper to wrap a piece of cheese in or hold it against their arm, twist it to create a paper cone, and put dry goods into that cone.

Several years later, the store underwent a major redesign. The whole shopping concept was altered. They eliminated salespeople on the floor and converted the store into what everybody called "a store without a shop assistant." All the merchandise was placed on shelves along the walls. Everybody got their own groceries and proceeded to the checkout. Gone were the mirrors, vases, and marble countertops. I have often wondered about the whereabouts of those gorgeous vases since then.

As the years went by, selections of products became scarce. Many varieties of food became rare or simply disappeared, and shelves remained empty. Lines of buyers became a regular sight. People would line up to buy such staples as butter, sugar, cheese, and fresh meat. People lined up for anything that was sold on a given day.

In Soviet lingo, this process of buying was called *getting*. You didn't *buy*, you *got*, maybe for a rainy day. You never knew. The process of selling something that called for long lines was called *giving out* or *handing out*. It was quite common for somebody to come up to the line and ask those in the line what the store was giving out. Such a convoluted euphemism for something so straightforward and simple as selling and buying was readily understood only in that part of the world.

In Soviet Georgia, farmers markets were a saving grace, as they were the place to go for fresh and organic food. Farmers markets operated every day of the week and were like huge grocery stores. There was a big farmers market not far from the city center, very close to our house, where Mom loved to go shopping. Even though the market was open daily, Mom went there on the weekends.

It was a two-story building where greens and vegetables were sold on the ground floor. The fruit, nuts, dried fruit, spices, flour, meat, fish, and poultry departments were upstairs. The ground floor was dimly lit, and the concrete floor was always wet, as the vegetable sellers watered their greens to freshen them up and even washed their vegetables right there near the counters.

The majority of greens and vegetable sellers were Azeri farmers from East Georgia. Mom sometimes haggled if the price seemed exorbitant. Azeri women farmers, who were always very friendly, spoke some Russian and very limited Georgian. Mom knew useful words in Azeri for conducting the transaction. She would start selecting eggplants or potatoes and would tell the farmer that she was looking for *yahshi* (good) or *choh yahshi* (very good) produce in the Azeri language.

These women farmers had gold front teeth that sparkled when they smiled and garish headscarves. They wore big bloomers, in the long legs of which they kept their money. Mom told me not to stare when they would slightly lift their skirts to stash the money we paid for our purchases or retrieve change literally from their underwear or from some hidden breast pocket. Their herbs and vegetables were usually fresh and luscious: parsley, cilantro, basil, oregano, tarragon, radishes, eggplant, green beans, cucumber, cabbages, tomatoes, and potatoes.

I preferred going upstairs, where the space was open and less crowded. A local butcher was Mom's acquaintance and Dad's former patient or a relative of a patient. I called him Uncle Malkhaz. He did not look like a butcher to me at all. He was a tall, slender man, kind-faced and friendly, always with a smile and cheerful greeting. He wore a white hat and a white apron, albeit smeared with blood. Later, when my parents had German shepherds, some of the best-quality bones for them came from this butcher.

I loved stalls with dried fruit and spices that emanated enticing aromas. Coriander, fenugreek, oregano, barberry, dried parsley, basil, celery, and many more were displayed in neat cotton sacks. The sellers themselves were neat and tidy ladies who selected spices carefully and with advice on how to use them in food. They measured spices meticulously in little cups and then poured them into small paper cones stacked on the counter. I was always fascinated by these cones, because they were made of pages from exercise notebooks or old textbooks, and I wondered who had recycled and folded them.

Seasonal fruit selections created multicolor aromatic displays. Some of them had very short shelf-life, and if picked ripe, they were further damaged during transportation. Ripe peaches and pears were easily bruised. If peaches were too ripe, they were usually sold by midmorning. It was always better to go to the market as early as possible to make the best selections.

In my mind's eye, I keep snapshots of neat piles of handpicked pears, strawberries, cherries, sour cherries, figs, apricots, persimmons, and apples. All of them were mouthwatering and delicious. Grapes would come toward the end of summer from the Kakheti region in East Georgia. These amber grapes were dense and fragrant with the nostalgic flavor of Georgian fall. Sometimes if we were invited to the grape harvest in somebody's vineyard, we would bring home with us branches of grapes and hang them in the kitchen to dry out for later consumption.

Years later, an unknowledgeable and uninformed language supervisor at the Foreign Service Institute in Washington, DC, told me it was not necessary to teach American diplomats Georgian cultural realities, as they only needed to be able to ask in Georgian how to get to the market and buy potatoes—to which I replied that this would be a blunder, as potatoes were not a Georgian staple food and diplomats would only expose their ignorance.

When Mom was shopping, we had to stay close to her and not wander away. In case we were separated, we had to stay put and not move. This directive was inculcated in us, and we followed it to a T. It became even more compelling after Mom once lost Gogi in a department store.

Gogi was in his first year of elementary school then. His school was within walking distance from our house, and the department store was en route. So after picking up Gogi from school, Mom dropped by the department store with Gogi in tow.

We were at home when Mom came back very worried and tearful. She had lost Gogi. She had been talking to the shop assistant and had let Gogi's hand go. She had looked everywhere in the store, but he was not to be seen. By that time, she was upset and frightened. She had decided to go home in case he had headed there, since he knew the way home and it was really very close. As he was not there, her anxiety grew.

By this time, everybody was concerned. Obviously, we couldn't sit and wait. We had to search for him. Mom was on her way out when I stepped onto the balcony to scout the street one last time. And there he was, striding home in his school uniform and cap, looking very serious and composed. He was more worried that he would be punished for wandering away than afraid of being lost.

Apparently, he had wandered away and got distracted. Then he started looking for Mom but could not see her. So he decided to come straight home. Theirs was a tearful reunion with dressing down, chiding, and hugs all in one, plus future instructions and promises that if we got separated from our parents, we had to stay put and wait for them to come and get us.

The department store was demolished several years later, replaced by a more modern construction for a better shopping experience. That building also fell victim to the whim of nouveau riche newcomers and their taste for newer concrete monstrosities that devoured the old downtown.

Four

MY GRANDPARENTS

My mom's parents lived in a spacious apartment in a charming district of Tbilisi called Vera. It was a quaint old district with crooked cobblestone streets that crawled up into Mount Mtatsminda, while the lower part of the district displayed more European sophistication and quiet elegance. You could reach my grandparents' street from different directions; one was by going up the steep street, which became perilous during snowy days. We had to cling to buildings while crawling down a slippery slope covered with treacherous patches of black ice.

Theirs was a quiet cul-de-sac at the foot of the mountain. Their family room had a fabulous panoramic view of the city spreading below it in recognizable patterns of streets and buildings. In the summer, the window was always open, letting in the breeze and distant rumble of the city below.

The apartment was my grandparents' happy world—sunny, airy, and very welcoming and comfortable. My sweet grandma and grandpa were Sylvia Mujiri and Benedicte (Beno) Baramidze, but we called them Bebe and Babu. My grandmother was a medical doctor. My grandfather was a historian. They were good professionals and fabulous grandparents.

Sylva, as she was known to her family and friends, must have been a beauty in her younger days. I remember her hair—already dark grey and completely white toward the end of her life—arranged in a little bun at the nape. She never wore any jewelry, only a wristwatch.

Grandma's nature was a fortunate combination of grace, delicacy, and bubbling energy. She was of a medium height and slender. Always swift, efficient, and attentive, no matter how tired she was, my grandma would whip up either *khachapuri* (our favorite cheese bread), pancakes, or cookies whenever we visited. She would never let us leave without giving us a treat.

Grandpa was our source for historical facts and dates regarding the ancient world, wars, and historic personalities. When I took Latin in my freshman year at the university and read Julius Caesar's *De Bello Gallico*, my grandpa surprised me with passages from the chronicle that he had committed to memory in his student years. It was not just the text that he remembered; he also launched into a discussion on the narrative and the events described in the book.

My great grandfather—my grandfather's father, Giorgi (equivalent to the English George) Baramidze—was a parish priest in West Georgia. He and his beautiful wife, Sonia Imnadze, had seven children. My grandfather was the eldest of them. He had three younger brothers, one of whom, Vano, died quite young from the Spanish flu, a pandemic that raged at the start of the twentieth century, taking many lives. He also had three sisters, one of whom, Nina, was also my godmother.

As the eldest son, my grandpa was expected to follow his father's footsteps and go into the priesthood. He was sent to Tbilisi Seminary. However, after graduating from the seminary, he decided to continue his studies at Tbilisi State University and major in history. He and his younger brother, Alexandre, rented an apartment and attended classes at the university.

Those were fruitful years for my grandpa. The classes in history, classical studies, and linguistics were taught by famous scientists and authors. The auditoriums were always packed with not only the students but also the general public that attended the fascinating lectures. I think it was from those leading masters that my grandpa acquired a knack for storytelling and factual analysis, which kept his audience equally spellbound.

My grandpa's formative years were closely intertwined with the historic events that befell Georgia at that time. After two hundred years of suffering under Russian expansion and conquest, Georgia declared independence in 1918, following the October socialist revolution in Russia. However, after three years of relatively agreeable relations between the Georgian Republic and Soviet Russia, the latter reneged on the treaty between the two and, in February of 1921, attacked the nascent republic.

My grandpa was a university student then. Along with hundreds of students, he enlisted to defend his Motherland. Georgia lost in fierce battles raging on the outskirts of Tbilisi. Russia's victory was swift and brutal. Thousands of Georgian lives were lost in the ferocious fighting. The outcome for the country was equally devastating. The Soviet regime was established throughout the country. Students, traumatized and heartbroken, picked up their lives and continued with their studies. My grandpa resumed his classes at the university.

I loved moving in with my grandparents at the end of the school year—not only because I was loved and pampered there but also because I found it immensely interesting to be around my grandparents. It was in their library that I read my favorite French writers: Victor Hugo, Alexandre Dumas, Honoré de Balzac, Guy de Maupassant, and Gustave Flaubert. I loved historical fiction. Reading about ancient kingdoms, wars, and battles was especially fascinating and safe in the comfort of the twentieth century Bebe-Babu sanctuary.

Grandma's parents, Anton Mujiri and Martha Glonti, were prominent and well-respected citizens in Ozurgeti, a town in West Georgia. Anton Mujiri had a good library and could recite long passages from *The Knight in the Tiger's Skin*, our national literary treasure, an epic poem by Shota Rustaveli, a twelfth-century poet. With this background, it is not a surprise that the scholarly tradition continued in my grandparents' household as well.

I remember discussing books with my grandparents. Grandpa always launched into a lengthy analysis of historical events, which I always found educational and captivating. Grandma and I shared books. If she napped with a book in her hands and eyeglasses on her nose, I knew it was time to nip it. Usually, it was a book that I also wanted to read. I would tiptoe and take it quietly while she had it in her hands with glasses on and eyes closed.

"I am not sleeping, Naniko," she would say. "I am reading."

One summer, the newly coveted book was *Jane Eyre*. I loved the book from page one and wanted to read it nonstop. I had competition, as my grandma was rereading her favorite passages in the book. The book itself had lost its hard cover long ago and was quite tattered.

"How many times do you have to reread it, Bebe?"

"It is a good book, dear."

That it was. The book was equally appreciated by a teenager and a mature reader.

It was there one summer that I discovered the world of Sir Arthur Conan Doyle. The stories were fascinating, scary, intriguing page-turners. I learned about the importance of deduction and analysis. That was a lifelong lesson for me and the beginning of a deep appreciation for mystery novels and whodunits. The very first story I read was "The Adventure of the Speckled Band" followed by "The Red-Headed League." The stories were in English and abridged, which made them easier for me to read.

Grandma was the head of the internal medicine department in the Transcaucasian Railway Hospital. Her workdays stretched long into the evenings.

"Why do you stay so late?" I would greet her in the hall when she returned home in the evenings.

"Well," she said, "my staff are all much younger, with families and small children, and they hurry home after work. I stay behind in case I am needed."

I attempted to counter that argument. "Surely there is a doctor on call if there is some emergency."

"In that case, I absolutely need to be there. You know I am in charge."

"Even when you have me staying with you?" I asked.

That was a feeble argument. It was no use looking for excuses. Even as a young teenager, I realized that Grandma's sense of duty and responsibility was something that even I had to take seriously. She gave me a lifelong lesson in a strong work ethic. She actually imbued it in me just by setting an example.

My dad respected her opinion when he, as a surgeon, needed the advice of an experienced internist. When we got sick, we always asked Mom to call Bebe to come and see us. Grandma would come after work and always had something yummy for a sick kid. She would wash her hands and sit at our bed, warming her stethoscope, and ask Mom to bring a spoon.

"Open your mouth, dear. Say ah!"

The handle of the spoon would press on the tongue. The stethoscope went on the back.

"Breathe in!" she would say. "Breathe out! Take a very deep breath!"

Sometimes she would simply put her ear to our backs to listen to our lungs or tap with her fingers. She always checked tonsils. Halfway through the exam, I usually felt much better, even if I was running a fever, simply because Grandma was there.

Grandpa worked in education. At different times, he was the head of the city education board, deputy head, and later a school principal before he retired. He also taught history. History was his passion, and conveying his love for it was his goal. A person of high moral principles, he was fair-minded and objective with his colleagues and students. An eager story-teller, he had us as his keen audience when he recounted historical events.

"And then what happened?"

"Why do you think it happened?"

"When exactly was that?"

"How many were they?"

These were questions from us, the eager audience, as we did not like to be left in suspense in the Middle Ages.

Modern Georgian history was especially fascinating to us, as those events were never chronicled the way they actually happened. Soviet propaganda took care of that. We already understood double standards and biased presentations. Babu had lived through those days—the purges of the twenties and thirties, the victims and survivors—which held special interest for me. We wanted to know how the people coped with all this. How did they survive? How did the society function? What did the life of an ordinary person look like?

Here is one of his stories. I think it was right before the Second World War. Grandpa was the head of the city education board when the principal of one of the schools asked to meet with him—as it turned out, to hand over a letter of resignation. This surprised my grandpa. The explanation was even more surprising, as well as traumatic.

"I cannot take it anymore!" was how the principal started. Some students at the school where he worked were children of Soviet party bosses. Coming from such a privileged background, these pampered students claimed to be the crème de la crème and expressed no regard for fellow students—or their elders, for that matter. After classes, they would march into the principal's office, ignoring the stunned secretary, to pick up the phone and summon their family driver to take them home. Nobody dared say anything.

The last straw was when, one day, these guys started kicking a bun as a football during recess. Their stunned classmates watched standing in semicircle. One of them fainted.

"I have kids who are malnourished," said the principal. "Some come from the purged families of political prisoners. They had not eaten good food for days, and to see a bun being kicked as a football was too much for one of them," concluded the principal.

Grandpa reported the incident at the meeting of the city council and got demoted himself. That was Soviet justice: party bosses were untouchable. As Grandma aptly stated, "I am happy he was just demoted and not sent to prison himself."

When Grandpa retired, he became an avid gardener at our country house. He also planted a concord grapevine below his balcony in Tbilisi. The vine crawled up and covered the entire balcony. Dark purple grapes provided aromatic shade in the summer and were pleasing to the eye. He even made wine out of the juice of these grapes. Red Concord wine is indeed delicious, with a very distinctive taste.

Grandpa's birthdays are worth mentioning here. His birthday was in December, and all his brothers and sisters would bring their families to wish him a happy birthday. It was a big and cheerful gathering, with kids running around and grown-ups talking or making toasts. There was always much noise and mirth.

My grandparents' dining room was spacious enough to accommodate all the guests, but we usually ran out of chairs and had to borrow from the neighbors. Somebody once joked that "in order to fit all the Baramidze family members, you need two tramcars."

I loved those gatherings when I could catch up with relatives of my own age and have fun. Grandma, the best cook I had ever known, usually turned these days into gala occasions. The feast was abundant with roast suckling pig, roast chicken, turkey in walnut sauce, fish, numerous vegetable entrees, pastries, and desserts.

As I grew older, I became more interested in the table conversations at these gatherings. My godmother, Nina, was a lawyer. Grandfather's younger brother, Alexsandre, was a scholar and a literary critic. He was also the director of the Institute of Literature, a place where literary critics, translators, and other literary scholars worked. Another brother, Michael, was a colonel in the army. They were captivating people with thought-provoking stories. Equally amusing were their children, my parents' generation.

These happy evenings linger in my memory and never fade away. Among the guests were Grandma and Grandpa's adopted son, known to us kids as Uncle Grisha. He was from the town of Poti, the port on the Black Sea. There is an interesting story connected to him. This happened in the late thirties when a group of educators from Tbilisi was sent to Poti on a business trip. Grandpa was among them. They stayed in a hotel. There was a little boy who volunteered to clean their boots and run errands. Since the visit took place during the school year, my grandpa got curious as to why this boy was not at school and why his parents were not around.

The little boy, who was very polite and courteous, respectfully replied, "I am an orphan. I don't have anybody. I seldom attend school. I am allowed to come and help around at the hotel."

Grandpa did not give it much thought. He did not even consult my grandma. But when he returned home, the little boy, Grisha Khabuliani, was with him. He stayed with the family for many years, graduating from school and college.

He became an engineer and returned to Poti. He married a nice lady from his hometown and had a very good family that often visited my grandparents. When Uncle Grisha happened to be in Tbilisi on a business trip, he would stay with my grandparents. He always dropped by to visit with us as well, as he adored my mother.

He was a quiet man with a smiling face and very kind blue eyes. He often brought dry mullet from Poti, and we all loved it. In his adult years, doctors discovered he had tuberculosis, likely as a result of his harsh childhood, and he had to be hospitalized for a short period of time.

My mom's younger sister Lia and brother Malkhaz, my favorite aunt and uncle, lived with my grandparents as well. They had stories about Mom taking care of them during the war when Grandma spent most of her time in the hospital and Grandpa was at war.

The Germans never reached Tbilisi, even though it was Hitler's intention to reach the strategically important Transcaucasus region with its Black Sea coast and the Caspian Sea oil. The Germans could not cross the Caucasus mountains. Despite that, Georgia was much involved in the war effort, and the country's hospitals were overflowing with the wounded sent down there to recuperate. Because of the hospital load and patient needs, my grandma was very busy, and that explained her absence from home.

Mom and her siblings were often on their own. Mom, who was in high school then, assumed the full responsibility of running the household and taking care of her younger siblings. They in turn absolutely adored their elder sister and listened to her without questioning her authority.

They lived through air raids and blackouts. When air raids would start, the kids, though left alone, knew exactly what to do. They went to the basement of their apartment building along with other neighbors in a very orderly and organized way, each carrying something useful and essential in case they had to stay there for long: a lamp or a candle, a bag full of small pieces of toasted bread, water, and books and notebooks so they could to do their homework. Years later, Mom heard me memorizing a poem for my Georgian class assignment, and she told me that she'd learned that one by candlelight in the basement during an air raid.

Lia is a chemist and was a professor at Tbilisi State University in the department of organic chemistry before she retired. She was working on her doctoral dissertation during a couple of summers that I spent at my grandparents' place. Malkhaz was an accomplished archeologist. He visited often and kept some of the discovered objects in his room while he worked on the scientific paper. I was instructed never to touch any of these objects.

He had to number and give detailed descriptions of the pieces of the clay jars. I watched how he glued ancient pieces together. There were other objects as well: beads, earrings, and bangles from burial grounds.

Most of Malkhaz's work, including his doctoral dissertation, was dedicated to archeological sites in Abkhazia in West Georgia. Once I even saw specks of real gold wrapped in a piece of cotton, which he showed me before taking it to the museum. I regret I never volunteered to go with him on archeological expeditions. Malkhaz was full of stories about the ancient finds. He authored many scientific articles and several books, some of which were published much later and even posthumously.

It was such a joy to listen to my grandpa, a historian, and my uncle, an archeologist, talk about the ancient history of Georgia. Yes, my grandparents' home was indeed a special place.

Five

MOM

Gamarjoba, deda![1]

You know, Mom, when I was an undergraduate student in Moscow, I received many letters from home. Sometimes I would not open letters from you for a day or two and would carry them in my bag unopened instead. I did that to have something to look forward to in anticipation of a special treat.

It was such a thrill to recognize your handwriting on an envelope. Your calligraphy was as comforting as your personality. I often tried to emulate your handwriting but could not keep up with the roundness of letters and their evenly measured simplicity. Reading letters so far from home gave me comfort and encouragement, from the endearments in salutations (*"Chemo Naniko"*[2]) to the hugs and kisses at the end—and your comforting presence in between.

You wrote about Dad, Gogi, and Revaz; friends and relatives; your work; events that you attended; and everything you knew I missed. You eased my nostalgia. In one of the letters, you joked that I finally taught you how to write long letters. Indeed, I had asked you to write more about everything, and you complied.

It was you who supported me in my decision to transfer to Moscow State University. You said it would be good for my character, and it

---

[1] Hello, Mom!

[2] My Naniko

was. It was not easy to get adjusted, but as it turned out, the overall experience there toughened me. It was not easy to move to a world so different from what I was used to—so cold and unfamiliar. Both you and Dad taught us the importance of self-reliance, which ultimately helped me to be independent and make my own decisions.

You were always there when you thought I needed advice. What was especially precious was your willingness to show me how proud you were of me. We had an understanding and a friendship. I disobeyed you only once—and in a very major way—when I told you and Dad that my life was mine to live, and I had met the love of my life. Later, how brave you were to concede defeat and in good spirits magnanimously shared our happiness in an elated and graceful manner. All this was in your generous letter, the letter to live by. Mom, I kept the letter, as I did all the other letters before and after that one.

The first night of your funeral, Rusiko Janashia[3] told me something I never knew—that your own family worried about you marrying Dad because they were not sure how your life would be with somebody who had a physical disability. You refused to listen to them and presented stronger arguments that he was a good man and you loved each other. Some of these were familiar arguments, almost verbatim repeating my own. I wish I had known that before.

Eventually, you prevailed over their fear. You and Dad were both so right to stick together. You created a happy family. Your love manifested itself every day, even in minute details like when Dad peeled a peach and cut it for you because you could not eat the skin of your favorite fruit, or offered you a piece of pear or apple and when you refused, said, "I made a wish for you to eat it, my Medea."

I remember how you took care of his needs, especially when his leg was hurting him; how you stood behind him during every challenge and decision. You had his back, and he knew it. Dad cherished and respected you. He became a lost man after you were gone. He lost not only his soulmate but his sense of direction.

By the time we left for America, you had been gone two years. We

---

[3] Rusiko Janashia was my mom's cousin twice removed. Rusiko's father, Simon Janashia, was a famous historian. The Georgian Central Museum of History and Ethnography is named after him. He was Grandma Sylva's cousin.

did not take much from home—hardly anything the first passage over. But I took your letters as part of home and a good omen. I guess I was lucky, because I had been away from home for a period of time, so I had accumulated quite a number of letters. In today's era of electronic communication, so much would have been lost. I imagine how our letters would be so unpardonably succinct and would lack character and voice. Rereading those letters that you and I shared now brings back moments long gone but never forgotten.

In one of the letters, you wrote that when you thought of me, you remembered how I cried when we read a story of two nestlings who were too young to leave their nest but felt adventurous enough to venture into the world. One day, they flew away and got lost. It started to rain. Hungry, wet, and shivering under a drainpipe, they cried that their mom was sweet and their home was warm and cozy. They knew it had been a mistake to fly away, and they wanted to go back. I cried with them, because I was sorry for the birds and afraid that their mom could not find them, but she did. I remember how I clung to you, thinking that you too were sweet and our home was warm and comfortable, and it could rain or snow outside, but we were safe inside with you.

Numerous moments of us being together are gone forever, but they remain in my subconscious and guide me in my actions every day of my life, never fading, never receding. Often when I get into myself, my thoughts lead to you. Now I want to recapture and revive what we had together and convey that magical comfort here, same as when I open the wardrobe where your dresses still hang and the subtle fragrance of you still lingers. How many times I hugged those dresses and inhaled you.

You are my frame of reference for motherly love. I often wonder how you managed to love us all equally and yet single out each of us for our remarkable qualities and our special place in your heart. Coming from a long line of very strong women, you could be very strict and demanding. One look from you was enough for us to be on our best behavior. I was often more afraid of you than I was of Dad. You somehow managed to love us kids without pampering or spoiling us.

What pains me most of all is that you cannot see how good my daughters are and how they emulate you now that they have their own families and children—your great grandchildren, Mom, born here in the United States and speaking Georgian.

You were my first reader of school papers, as I trusted your literary taste and fair judgment. It is from you that I got my love for the written word. The number of poems that you could recite from memory was astounding. Reading to us when we were kids was your favorite pastime. How much we read, Mom! Nursery rhymes, poems, Greek myths and legends, fairy tales—some were so scary that I sat close against you seeking safety and comfort.

I still remember what made me cry and shiver. Long before Walt Disney created Bambi, Georgian children had *The Tale of a Fawn of the Doe* by Vazha Pshavela. I see myself pressing up against you and holding my breath in scared anticipation, listening to the tale of a little orphan fawn whose mom was killed by a hunter. Oh, how I hated hunting and rifles. When you read to us, I leaned into you and shared your warmth.

Our first books were *The Wedding of Jay Birds, Little Donkey Muffin and His Friends, Katie Is Dressing Herself,* and *The Sleeping Beauty.* So many of my first absolute favorite books from those days, my loyal friends and companions, are now frayed, dog-eared, and torn, glued and sewn together. Some survived because you kept them for me. I read to my grandchildren those very books, reliving the happy moments of my childhood. Thank you, Mom, for this as well.

One of the books you liked best was *David Copperfield.* It soon became my favorite too. We were both sorry for little Davy and his mom and shared loyalty with characters that we both found kind and agreeable. Sometimes to better describe someone, you said that the person was a typical Uriah Heep. So often this was a most appropriately applied adjective, and I knew exactly what you meant.

I do not remember any parental platitudes from you. As a matter of fact, I don't remember you launching into a lengthy discussion on good and bad. Instead, you taught by example. When I grew up, we argued a lot, as I always wanted to prove my point. You generously accepted my point, or other times we declared a truce.

With your image come your hands, Mom—smart hands that created magic around us, strong and warm hands wearing no jewelry. You seldom wore even your wedding band, only a watch. When I was sick, I remember your hand checking my forehead and stroking my head. My earliest memories are of those hands holding books and reading to us.

You took pride in having a very clean and tidy household. Those hands cleaned and washed, cooked and baked, and knitted beautiful sweaters. Evenings in front of a TV for you were seldom wasted without you doing something constructive.

You were an excellent cook and a great baker. Your Easter cake was something we all looked forward to. The aroma of vanilla and cardamom permeated the house, lingering for days. In true Easter spirit, you baked several cakes at once to give to relatives and neighbors. That was your Easter tradition. The first night when you passed away, Revaz's friend Vano said, "No more Easter cakes from now on."

The first Easter after you were gone, I attempted to recreate your Easter magic and baked Easter cake using your recipe. It was a serious undertaking for me—since, as you know, I am rather heavy-handed when it comes to baking, and also the process of preparing and making that particular dough is tedious and requires attention to detail. I realized that Easter cake is temperamental and can easily come out flat. You know how I could not follow recipe instructions.

My first Easter cake tasted less sweet, as I forgot to add enough sugar. Despite that, it still came out quite good. Everybody loved it. Dad said, in his usual encouraging way, that we were not sending it to a baking competition, and even if we were, it would get a prize for being so pretty and yes, tasty too, and too much sugar was not good for us anyway. Indeed, the dough rose well and was delicate and fluffy. I have been baking Easter cakes every Easter now. One more of your many legacies, mom.

Memories are suspended in time and frozen by frames. Often when I think about you, what comes to mind is you standing in the doorway of the apartment in Moscow where I lived during my college years. You had just arrived, standing there in your coat and hat, happy to see me and bringing home with you.

Once you said that home is where a mother is. The poignant truth of this statement hit me hardest on the day when you were gone. You indeed personified home. You were that binding power that kept us all together, happy and safe.

It was your decision to have Dad's cousins Iza and Tina live with us while they were in college. You welcomed them and created a home for them as well. We were one big happy family, all of us living together. Then when Iza became a medical doctor and Tina a chemical engineer, you were so proud of their achievements—but they had a good role model in you, Mom!

Everybody who knew you loved and respected you. All the relatives just adored you. Your colleagues at work appreciated and trusted you. You had a certain quiet charm which easily won others over.

When you passed away, Dad received a letter of condolence from Kirill Lange[4]—a warm and cordial letter from somebody who knew you both well, having spent a considerable amount of time with you in St. Petersburg. He wrote that everything Dad had achieved was thanks to you, your sense of purpose, your strength and moral support, and your willingness to always stand by Dad. All so true. I still don't know how being such a gentle person you exerted so much strength, will, and determination.

All that Gogi, Revaz, and I have achieved in our lives, we owe to you. You somehow managed to be infinitely proud of us without ever indulging us. Sure, there were times when each of us could be whimsical or erratic, but you knew how to deal with that behavior. And you knew when it was okay to give in to childish demands.

You told me a story about how once when I was little and at the St. Petersburg Zoo, I was fascinated by ponies. As the zoo was offering rides, I tearfully pleaded with you to let me have a ride on a pony. Apparently, I cried in Russian, "I want a pony!" You let me have a ride.

I don't remember any of this. Neither do I remember that a nosy bystander, a Russian lady in a mentoring tone, chastised and rebuked you for letting me have my way. "Today she requested to have a pony, tomorrow she will demand to have a Pobeda." She was referring to the Soviet car model, the latest rage of fashion. I can just see you in my

---

[4] Kirill Lange was my father's colleague in the Institute of Physiology in St. Petersburg.

mind's eye being lectured by a complete stranger and being too nice-mannered to respond. You probably just smiled at her.

You hated hurting other people's feelings, whether an adult or a child … but especially a child. I remember once when you arrived in Moscow, you stood in the kitchen at the cooking range. I came and hugged you, and you looked at Alyona,[5] who had entered the kitchen and sat there. You told me in Georgian that hugging in front of Alyona, who missed her mom, was not right, and I stopped hugging you. You went and hugged Alyona. She really missed her parents, who were working in Stockholm.

During those last few months of us being together, when you were sick, one of the nurses from work sent you a card. I kept it. She wished you a speedy recovery and wrote "Get well soon, Dr. Mediko. We are going to go on curing patients together." You were brave those last days of your life. True to yourself, you never complained once, as you didn't want to bother us. All your life, you were used to helping others. You were there for your family, friends, patients, and neighbors. In your many good-hearted endeavors, you were always unassuming and gracefully generous.

Tamriko[6] told me later that you told her you were not afraid of death, but you were afraid of pain. You never shared those thoughts with me. Only once you told me that you saw your fear in my eyes. That was the only time you admitted to me that you were scared. How I wanted to reassure you then that all was okay. But it was not, and our world was crashing.

When we were growing up, we knew you were fair and strict and always commanded respect. You could get very angry and showed it too. I remember one day I misbehaved at school. I was six years old and in first grade. My friend Marina and I shared a desk and played there in between the class activities, even though playing was not allowed during lessons.

That day during math class, Marina and I played with little toys that

---

[5] Alyona was my landlady's daughter in Moscow. I rented a room in the apartment where she lived with her grandmother while her parents worked in Stockholm, Sweden. She was the same age as Revaz, and we treated each other as sisters.

[6] Tamriko Tourmanidze is my sister-in-law—Revaz's wife.

we had brought from home. We drew a dividing line between us on the bench to keep to our own space, but Marina crossed over, and I pinched her on the thigh. Meanwhile, the class was learning to write the number 4, and students were being called to go to the board to write the new number.

Marina raised her hand to tell on me. The teacher thought that she wanted to go to the board and told her to do so, but Marina said, "No. I raised my hand because Nana pinched me."

The teacher came closer to see what was going on and saw our toys. I still remember her anger, and I knew we were in trouble. Actually, I didn't like that teacher. I never got into her good graces, and she always found a reason to punish me and put me in the corner. That day, too, I was called in front of the class and ordered to stand in the corner.

How upset you were with me when the teacher told you that again I had misbehaved. On the way home, you told me that I would have to try to be good and listen to the teacher. "Trying is all it takes," you said. You and I were both miserable in our own ways that day.

Then one day, a miracle happened, and the teacher was pleased with me. I must have really tried to be a good girl. When you came to pick me up, I learned a new word: *brilliantly*. The teacher told you that I behaved brilliantly the whole day—that I didn't take my eyes off of her and listened to her every word. Since then, when I come across the word *brilliant*, I see your happy face listening to the praise.

As the school was near our house, we usually walked. There were two ways to get there. One was going down Rustaveli Avenue or going along the upper street, which then was called Dzerzhinski Street and later was renamed Pavle Ingorokva Street. I loved both routes, but the upper street was more interesting, because we had to go past a park that had lush vegetation and swans in a big pond. The park was part of the Pioneer Palace and could be accessed from the front gate. It was enclosed by a cast iron fence, and I loved looking inside at the tranquil beauty. We often stopped on our way to admire the swans and beautiful flowers.

Years later, the park would be destroyed, and a government building would be built there instead. Some beautiful houses would be torn down as well. At the spot where the swans lived, an ugly monument of Lenin sitting in an armchair would be erected—a true eyesore. You were already gone, Mom, and didn't know that the swans had their revenge in the nineties when the national liberation movement started and the repulsive monstrosities of the Soviet era were dismantled. The sitting leader was cast away as well.

Those hazy days of my childhood are concealed in distance. They are far away and sweet and precious. They carry the flavor of my childhood. Some of the memories are fading, but others vividly stand out and remind me not to forget that little girl and her mom walking home hand-in-hand; not to disappoint them, not to betray their friendship, not to forget their conversations, hopes, and promises. I feel your presence today as if you had never let go of my hand.

Many years later, I came across these words by Kate Douglas Wiggin: "Most all the other beautiful things in life come by twos and threes, by dozens and hundreds. Plenty of roses, stars, sunsets, rainbows, brothers and sisters, and aunts and cousins, but only one mother in the whole world." I was fortunate to have you.

I am ever so grateful to you for many things and many memories but most importantly for your sense of decency and noble aspirations, for encouraging us to always hold ourselves to higher standards, and for the significance of loyalty that you imbued in us.

Love,
Your Nana

Six

DAD

It is easy to write about my dad, Giorgi Bochorishvili or Batoni Gogi.[7] It is also difficult because there is so much I would want to capture and relay here. Dad was ninety-two years old when he passed away. He outlived Mom by twenty-one years.

Charismatic is the word that comes to mind when I think about him—extraordinary and memorable. He was someone you would notice immediately and single out in a crowd.

Dad walked with a limp and used a cane. He preferred not to use it, but it was safer with the cane. His walk added to his personality a special significance, which was dignifying and noble at the same time. He did not just come into a room—he made an entrance and would immediately command attention. He was gregarious and dashing, impressive, and important. He loved meeting people and striking up conversations.

His social circle was wide, and he enjoyed being popular. He had big dreams and expressed himself expansively. Dad even wrote in big letters. Large, upright letters marched across a page in confident rows. Over a period of time, I received quite a number of letters from him. All of them were declarations of love, blessings, encouragement, advice, and pride.

Dad had a winning smile and a compelling personality. He loved the color red, and red ties were his absolute favorites. He was a fighter and a

---

[7] *Batoni* means "Mister" in Georgian. *Gogi* is short for Giorgi (George).

41

survivor. His opinion carried weight, and he was much respected by his colleagues and loved by his students.

As a self-made man, he was confident without being arrogant and friendly without being presumptuous. He had learned long ago from his own grandparents that one had to work hard to succeed in life, no matter the obstacles. He inculcated that wisdom in his own children.

He abhorred indolence. If he was told that somebody was talented, he would ask, "Is he hard-working as well? Because talent without work is wasted." I have never met anyone as hard-working as he was. If not in a clinic, Dad was working on his books. He was always busy, always with a sense of purpose.

My early years are full of recollections as to how my dad worked in his study at home. He was always either writing a textbook, editing a paper, or working with a graduate student. Academic medicine was as important to him as practicing surgery. He was constantly honing his skills, trying to catch up with the latest research and discoveries. When my daughter became a student at a medical school in the United States, my dad was understandably proud and happy. He wanted to know all about the curriculum, classes, and teaching methods. His insatiable desire to learn something new never seemed to waver.

He authored more than twenty-one textbooks and around a hundred scientific papers. It was general knowledge unanimously repeated by physicians that my dad was not just a brilliant surgeon but an excellent diagnostician as well. He also had this amazing knack for empathy, probably because he knew firsthand about pain and suffering. He pioneered many medical projects and introduced innovative ways of treating some conditions.

Dad was an absolutely fabulous speaker, full of humor and interesting stories as well as solid advice, professional tips, and pointers. He never read from his notes. He would prepare for a public presentation thoroughly and well in advance but never read his speech. He said that you had to look at your audience and establish rapport. He excelled at this. It's one of many skills that I learned from him. I also never read from my notes. In his speeches, he always sounded credible. Students loved him and aspired to be as good as him—worthy of his praise.

Always promoting a healthy way of life, he was the first to set an example. He was a big advocate for healthy eating and physical exercise.

"Eat little and exercise."

"You must leave the table still feeling a little hungry."

"Eat more fruit and vegetables, nuts, less baked goods."

Even when we were kids, Dad never forced food on us. When we were little and Mom was on call and had to go to the hospital, she would leave a cooked meal for Dad to feed us. One evening, he asked us if we were ready to eat.

We said, "No, not hungry yet."

Dad left us alone and didn't ask again. The next day, when Mom looked at the almost untouched food, she asked Dad what had happened.

Dad replied, "Well, I asked the kids if they were ready to eat. They replied they were not hungry. So I left them alone. They didn't ask for anything later either. I guess they were not hungry."

All the latest worldwide enthusiasm for organic food and healthy eating had been the lifestyle in our household forever. Dad hated cigarette smoking, and those who were aware of this knew better than to smoke when Dad was around.

As a surgeon, Dad was a risk taker. He often operated on patients whose chances of recovery were tenuous, but taking a risk was often worth it. He just didn't like to lose and was always hopeful, fighting until the end. He was superstitious when it came to his patients. He would never say that all was well until his critical patient was indeed on the mend.

He was crushed by Mom's illness and seriously defeated for the first time. He could not get over the fact that while he had saved so many lives, saving the most important life was beyond his medical expertise and power. In those days when Mom lay in their bedroom in our country house, I saw Dad downcast and overcome for the first time. This was when Revaz took over and took charge of taking care of Mom.

Revaz and Gogi before him followed in Dad's footsteps and went into medicine. They both were Dad's students, and he groomed them well for their future profession. Dad was demanding and tough and expected a lot from them. As time showed, he would not be disappointed in either of them.

Gogi holds a doctoral degree and is a urologist. He is the leading specialist at the National Center of Urology in Tbilisi and a participant in multiple international conferences worldwide. A Fulbright scholar, he also worked at Sloan Kettering Memorial Hospital in New York.

Revaz, also an MD PhD, became a general surgeon, but after Mom passed away, he decided to honor her by switching to ob-gyn to follow in her footsteps taking care of women's health. He combined two specialties and is now a consultant gynecologist at Estaing University Hospital and director of the International Training Center for Endoscopic Surgery in Clermont-Ferrand, France.

Dad did not like us to be disrespectful toward others, even when we were just kids. I remember once when I was still in grade school, sitting in Dad's car, I pointed out somebody in the street who was acting strangely and said, "Oh, there is a crazy man!" Dad launched into an admonition on how we should not be rude and discourteous and never say *crazy* but if that indeed was the case, to say *mentally ill* instead. I was maybe seven years old at that time, so a talk about mental illness was beyond my understanding, but Dad treated me like an adult and expected me to treat other people with respect even at that age.

Dad was indeed different, and not only because he had one leg. Actually, when I was growing up, I thought all adult men only had one leg. I remember how surprised I was when I first saw two-legged men at the Black Sea coast where we went for a summer vacation. I was probably four or five, and I asked Mom how come all these men had two legs and ran into water with so much ease, unlike Dad?

Dad took time to get into the water and usually stayed there for a long time. He loved the water and was an excellent swimmer. He could swim far away, and only his head would be visible like a little dot in the water. He learned to swim during childhood before he lost his leg.

One summer, we were in the countryside for our summer vacation in South Georgia. We had rented an apartment. Gogi and I spent a lot of time with the local kids. We usually played outside and rushed in and out of the house to grab a toy or drop something off, or rest, get a bite, do a bit of reading, and rush out again. There was a little local boy who befriended us and tagged along. He may have even been a son of our landlady.

One day, all three of us scrambled into our sitting room. We were too tired to play. It was hot outside, and we decided to sit inside and play some games. Suddenly, our little friend froze in the doorway. It was the first time I saw somebody visibly go completely white and shaken. He pointed with a trembling hand in the direction of Dad's prosthesis, which was propped up against a chair.

"What is that?" whispered the kid in a harsh, quivering voice.

"That's Dad's leg," Gogi answered, all nonchalant and matter-of-fact.

For us, it was a normal occurrence that Dad would take the prosthesis off at home to give his stump a rest and use crutches instead. For Gogi and myself, everything related to Dad's leg, or its absence rather, was taken for granted, and we didn't give it a second thought. For us, that was normal. However, the little boy suddenly remembered that his mom wanted him back home and dashed outside.

When we were very little, Dad would tell us stories from his childhood. One story was about a little black and white piglet who got lost, and Dad had to go and search for it. Every time he told the story, the piglet would get into more trouble and would make it harder for Dad to find him. The story about the piglet became our inside joke.

Dad had a harsh childhood. His family lived in Tkibuli, a coal-mining town in West Georgia. Dad adored his paternal grandparents, Ivlita and Pirran, because they were paramount in his upbringing. Their lives were shattered with the establishment of the Soviet regime in Georgia.

Dad was five years old when his father was arrested along with other patriots in West Georgia in 1924. They revolted against the Soviet takeover. This was the biggest and most well-organized uprising since the Soviet occupation of Georgia in 1921. The uprising was crushed fiercely and with a vengeance. Hundreds of people were arrested and imprisoned all over Georgia. A death sentence was the fastest verdict for them. When they rounded up hundreds more patriots in West Georgia, they threw them into a freight train and later executed them with submachine guns, without any trial, right there in an open field.

As Dad recalled, he and his grandfather Pirran went to a nearby village to visit relatives whose sons were among the executed and left unattended right where they were executed. It was a tragic day, which became even more tragic when the news reached my dad's grandfather that his son had also been arrested. Horrified, Pirran hastily headed home, taking a shortcut through the woods. Dad, who was five years old at the time, was terrified that he would be lost in the woods and tried to stay close, running after his grandfather.

The news was indeed grave. Dad's father, Bagrat, had been arrested along with other participants in the uprising. However, Bagrat's imprisonment did not last long. He became seriously ill in prison and was released to his family. He passed away very soon after his release. At that time, my grandmother, Nadya, was twenty-four years old, a pretty widow with two small kids—my dad and his younger sister, Mariam. Nadya never remarried and understandably felt resentment toward the Soviet regime all her life.

Dad's grandfather Pirran was branded an "undesirable element" and regarded with suspicion by the state. Soviet occupation proved to be a personal tragedy for Pirran's family. Once prosperous and happy, they were overcome with grief. Pirran's two sons fell victim to the Soviet occupation. Pirran and Ivlita lost their elder son as a result of the 1924 uprising and then several years later dad's uncle Levan was arrested as a Trotskyist and perished in the gulag. He never even had a chance to start a family.

As it turned out, my great grandparents did not even have time to mourn their loss, as they had to support their elder son's widow as best they could. Pirran was a *feldsher* by training—a paramedic who could practice in rural areas. For years, Pirran was the only paramedic practicing in several villages. These villages did not have a local doctor. A doctor would only visit them once a week. In the doctor's absence, Pirran took care of them. He was much respected by his countrymen.

With time, Pirran realized that he also had a good business sense. He gave up his medical practice and went into business. All this was happening at the turn of the twentieth century and before the Soviet occupation. He became quite a successful businessman. Pirran owned several stores that were very popular among the local population. He kept his money in Russian and Swiss banks.

However, with the Soviet takeover, the money was confiscated. Pirran lost everything. Dad remembered that there were so many voided checkbooks that he and his sister were allowed to play with them. Pirran was despised by the Soviet state, even though he had lost his sons, his stores, and his land. The family had to adjust to the new order and be extra cautious in their everyday lives.

In the early twenties, purges were rampant in Georgia. People had to be on the lookout. These were dangerous years for everyone. People were being arrested and executed without any reason. It was not just ordinary people but many famous scientists, actors, and artists. Many Georgian writers were also deemed undesirable by the state. Some of them were arrested or executed.

Vazha Pshavela, one of the greatest Georgian writers, had lost his son to the purges. The young man was executed for opposing the new regime and participating in the uprising. Naturally, his father fell under suspicion as well. Dad told us that if it so happened that they were reading a book by Vazha Pshavela and a neighbor dropped in, they had to hide the book, as nobody could be trusted. Reading a book by a forbidden writer was a punishable offence.

Dad was a good student. At that time, after completing grade school, students were required to have a referral from the local Soviet council to go to middle school. Dad went to pick up the referral but was told that they could not give a referral to him because his father and uncle were enemies of the people and his grandfather was a petit bourgeois. The State had to punish Dad and ostracize him from society.

The unfair decision upset the little boy, and he started to cry right there in the office. A stranger who happened to be in the council building took pity on him.

"He is an orphan," the stranger said. "All the neighbors see how he works and helps his family." The kindly gentleman concluded with the advice, "If he wants to study, we must not stand in his way."

He seemed to have some weight, as his interference helped with a favorable outcome. The chairperson's administrative assistant was also willing to help my dad. She immediately wrote a referral, which the chairperson had to sign. It turned out that the chairperson was illiterate. Instead of signing the letter of referral, he put a cross on the paper. These were the people who had come to power.

What the kind gentleman said was indeed true. Dad had worked all through his childhood, as he also had to help his mom and contribute his share. During summer vacations and sometimes after classes throughout the school year, Dad worked at a railroad depot. He helped workers unload cement or salt from freight trains. He fetched and carried for hours on end. He did not wear shoes, as wearing shoes in the summer was almost considered a luxury. Because he worked barefoot, salt burnt and irritated his feet. He did not cover his nose either, and cement inflamed his lungs and bronchi. He coughed up cement for days. Other times, he also worked at a lumbermill as a helper. The story of the piglet who got lost was a true story from those days when Dad worked as a herder.

Since his very early years, Dad had emulated his grandparents in hard work and perseverance. It took great tenacity and determination to rise above the grim reality and open hostility. Both Pirran and my dad looked at the reality for what it was: the stigma of a repressed family. They accepted the challenge and adapted to the new regime in order to survive and thrive.

Dad excelled in his studies so much that he was sometimes allowed to be a teacher's assistant. He graduated from high school with distinction and went on to medical school to fulfill his dream of becoming a medical doctor. In the Soviet Union, young people were allowed to go to medical school directly after graduating from high school. His skills of assiduity and hard work that were honed over the years helped him in college. He was soon noticed by his professors. Dad was especially honored and proud that Grigol Mukhadze, the famous surgeon, noticed and wanted Dad to work with him.

After graduation, Dad did not have much time to practice medicine, as he was conscripted into the army. It was April of 1942. The German forces entered the Soviet Union in June of 1941, and the Georgians, along with the peoples of all the republics within the Soviet Union, were drafted to defend the Soviet Union. Dad was twenty-three, fresh from medical school, a young surgeon still with two legs.

He was sent to Kerch Peninsula in eastern Crimea, where the fiercest battles took place at the time. On May 13, the field hospital where he was appointed came under brutal air attack. Dad remembered bits and pieces of what happened that day. They had to evacuate the wounded, and he was left in charge of this undertaking.

When the bombing started, he was still in the hospital. When he regained consciousness, Dad discovered that he had been wounded and was outside in the open field. His left shoulder was bleeding, but the worst pain came from his right leg, which appeared to have been torn away. It was hanging, barely clinging to the thigh bone, which was sticking out. This was a shell wound, fierce and brutal.

When he regained consciousness, Dad set out to save his own life. He always kept a needle with a thread in his surgical cap. He still had his cap on, and the needle and thread came in handy. He pulled out the thread and bound up the bleeding veins. He did not remember very well what happened next. The story emerged from another surgeon's notes. They found Dad unconscious. Even though he had stopped the heavy bleeding himself, they knew he could not survive without immediate surgical help.

The decision was reached immediately right there in the field. A door blown out from the building served as an operating table. Two boulders were cleaned with medical alcohol and iodine. The boulders were used to crush the protruding bone. The surgeons sawed away as much as they could of the bone and then stitched up and dressed the wound. Later, Dad was put on a little truck and sent to join the other wounded on a boat that was bound for the mainland.

What Dad remembered after he was sent away is equally amazing. The road came under constant air attacks. He saw a Messerschmitt that flew very close, almost reaching the ground. With each attack, the driver of the truck would run for shelter and jump into a ditch along the road, leaving Dad exposed. He lay on his back, stared at the sky, and helplessly watched the attack.

The German pilot and Dad locked eyes. Dad remembered the eyes of the pilot who would look at Dad, hover over, and fly away. Then he would return to hover over Dad again and fly away. Dad often wondered about the German pilot and how the man had spared his life. He speculated as to why he was spared. Was it because Dad looked so helpless when the driver would leave him behind? Maybe Dad reminded the pilot of somebody back home? Many maybes, a generous decision, and a miraculous outcome.

Dad survived. This is the shortest sentence that can contain all the emotional and physical pain, dismay, and crushing of dreams as well as the joy at being alive. His biggest fear was that he could not be a surgeon anymore—not with only one leg. However, his mentors and older colleagues encouraged him to get a prosthesis. And here again, perseverance triumphed, as if all his previous life he honed his skills to overcome this dilemma of a one-legged existence. This he regarded not even as a defeat but a mere setback.

Many years later, Konstantine Gamsakhurdia, a Georgian writer, met Dad in a publishing house and asked him why he walked with a limp. Dad explained. Mr. Gamsakhurdia mused, "In such a case, my mother would say, it is luck that you were hit by the calf and not the bull itself."

Dad became an assistant professor at the department of general surgery. Thus, his life as a surgeon started successfully and flourished with time. During this period, he met my mom, Medea Baramidze. She was a student in his class, and she fell in love with the young, handsome assistant professor who singled her out immediately as well. By that time, he was over thirty and was wary of who would want to connect her fate with him in his condition. But meeting Mom changed his life. Soon they started a family.

Dad started to work on his doctoral thesis. As was the tradition in the USSR, he first defended the candidate's dissertation. Several years later, he started work on his doctoral dissertation at the Pavlov Institute of Physiology in St. Petersburg. Gogi and I were very young then and spent our time between the two cities, Tbilisi and St. Petersburg.

When Dad returned to Tbilisi, he continued his work at the department of surgery at Tbilisi State Medical Institute as an associate professor and then a full professor. Later, he became the head of the general surgery department. During these years, he authored many scientific articles, books, and surgical manuals. He was an engaging speaker and a very dedicated educator. He emulated his great mentors Grigol Mukhadze, Michael Chachava, Egnate Pipia, and others, whom he always held in high regard. He was equally attentive to younger doctors, students, and graduate students. I remember many night phone calls to our apartment when Dad's expertise was needed at the clinic, and he would rush to help.

There were times when Dad's residual stump would start to hurt. It usually happened with the weather change. Mom joked that we had a live barometer at home. We knew several days in advance if it was going to rain soon or get cold; his limb would let us know. Sometimes the pain lasted several days, and Mom took care of him, administering pain medication and keeping him in bed. However, Dad almost never missed work because of the pain, especially if he had a planned surgery. Only his family members knew about the pain. Dad often saved lives standing for several hours operating on a patient while he himself was in pain.

As a surgeon, Dad did not like to amputate a limb unless it was indeed a life-threatening case and amputation was the last resort. He would say that he knew firsthand what it was like to live without a limb, and he would first fight to save it. I remember one night we went to see a performance at the Rustaveli Drama Theater. Parts of the theater were being renovated, and the main entrance was closed. Patrons had to enter from the side entryway. When our family approached the theater, I could see some men standing in the foyer talking. Suddenly, one of them saw Dad and rushed to the main entrance and opened it to let us in. He hugged Dad and greeted us. I had no idea who he was. I was embarrassed that everybody looked at us and wondered why we received VIP treatment.

The friendly gentleman turned out to be the head of the fire department at the theater and Dad's former patient. Dad had saved his arm, which had been severely damaged and would otherwise require urgent amputation. No wonder the gentleman was so happy to see Dad. This was one of many stories of grateful patients.

There were unfortunate outcomes too. As a rule, Dad did not like to lose, and to lose a patient was especially agonizing and distressing. Even after he retired from practice, he continued to teach and consult. He had too much knowledge and experience not to share it with students.

Dad had received medals from World War II, which he never wore. Once he went to a convention for the medical personnel who participated in World War II. He did not pin up medals to his suit but kept them on a string in his pocket. He did not like to show off his medals. I think he did not need to, as the limp itself was a medal, and Dad carried it gracefully all his life. Later in life, he also became a recipient of the Georgian Order of Honor.

Dad had a calming presence at home. I remember when I had a problem and shared it with him, he would gladly give his opinion. Often upon hearing my story, he would express his disapproval if he thought that I was unfairly treated, but first he attempted to minimize my own emotions with, "Ah! No! How is it possible! How can this be! Let's see …" It somehow helped that Dad shared my anger.

He usually had a calming effect on me even though at first, he would sound emotional himself. What I often needed was simply his presence and his support. And I always felt both.

Dad first tried his hand at a "therapy" with me many years earlier when I was little. I was maybe four when I started having nightmares about turkeys. I must have seen a turkey in the countryside. Actually, I think that's where I first saw a turkey and was mesmerized by the ugly snood hanging off its beak, as well as the whole neck and wattle, all a purplish gray mass which looked equally horrible. I stared at the turkey, it stared back at me, and then it gobbled loudly, finalizing my total disgust and fright.

After this encounter, it was not surprising that the ugly bird visited me in my nightmares. Every time I would scream in panic when I dreamed of a turkey—that it was in the room and my bed. No matter how they soothed and reassured me, the turkey was there to visit again at night.

One night when I woke up crying that I saw the turkey, Dad came to my bed, bent over, looked at the bed for a while, and said, "That is not a turkey at all. Look! It is Gogi's sock. Look at it! It is right there in the corner of your bed. Gogi must have dropped it here."

Sure enough, it was one of my brother's blue-gray socks—very familiar and not threatening at all. I held it in my hand as Dad suggested. I did wonder very briefly how Gogi's sock ended up in my bed, but I didn't question it. Then I closed my eyes and went back to sleep, never to dream of a turkey again.

Later, when I grew up, I realized what Dad did that night. He made me believe that what I was afraid of was a harmless little sock and nothing more. Many years later, I saw a wild turkey in the woods of North Carolina flying ponderously from one tree to another, but I didn't stare at it too long, even though it really looked harmless. Nobody would leave socks in my bed anymore.

A close friend once noted that despite my dad's image, it was my mom who ran the household and made decisions. That was true. Dad relinquished his rights to Mom in that regard. He fully trusted her judgment in everything, be it any decision that concerned the kids or even which furniture to buy. He let her buy it without even seeing it himself.

Dad was fascinated by America—her achievements and leadership, and also her role in the outcome of World War II. He was proud that we started to learn English at a very young age. He liked to parade our English skills whenever he had an occasion. We played along but refused to comply after a certain age.

The last one of these occasions was when a surgeon from a London hospital visited the clinic where Dad worked. It was a female surgeon—tall, gray-haired, and very lean. She had her own interpreter, but Dad wanted me to meet her also and act as his personal interpreter. I was in middle school then. The surgeon was pleased to hear me speak English, and we held a light conversation during lunch at the clinic.

I remember that year I had discovered George Byron, and on the spur of the moment decided to demonstrate my appreciation of English poetry. I started reciting the first lines from "Childe Harold's Pilgrimage": "Adieu, adieu! my native shore/Fades o'er the water blue …" That was too much showing off on my part. Reciting poetry so unexpectedly was out of place there in the clinic. The unsuspecting surgeon probably thought that I was preparing to leave. Or could it be that she did not share my love for poetry? She just kept smiling kindly. She gave me her card to drop in if ever I visited London. I kept the card for quite some time until it got lost.

My brothers and I emulated both of our parents and mirrored their way of life. We learned from an early age that hard work and persistence eventually pay off. We had to study well, read much, educate ourselves, and be fighters.

Dad was a little disappointed that I did not want to pursue a career in medicine and decided to major in English, but he stood by me in this decision. He was proud when I decided to transfer to Moscow State University, because he recognized himself in me. He was glad that I was not afraid to face challenges in life. I wanted to be independent and refused to be pampered. This side of my character made him especially happy.

In all his letters to me, he stressed the importance of hard work and determination. On one of the books that he gave me when I was already married, he wrote a dedication in his large straight letters: "To my Nana with love. Be blessed! May you have happiness with your husband and children. I wish you success and expect it from you. Dad"

Often when I am left alone with my thoughts, I seclude myself to the luminous place kept intact in my memory. It's Dad's study—the safest fixture of my childhood, a quiet welcoming room with Dad's desk against a wall lined with shelves from floor to ceiling. If I stand on the desk, I can climb up the nearest shelf to reach the top shelf with adult fiction like *Decameron* or *One Thousand and One Nights*. I can see myself banging on a typewriter with an index finger my first poem: "A bird is sitting in a tree, the bird is chirping." I am suspended in time there. The door that lets out onto the balcony is open. Of course it is open—to let the fresh air in. It was my dad's lifelong mantra: "Open windows to let fresh air in!"

There is a fireplace in the corner of his study built with gorgeous French tiles that Dad had rescued. They almost got destroyed after some construction workers tore down an old building in St. Petersburg. The tiles came from the fireplaces inside that building. Dad happened to come across the site quite by chance, as it was next to the building where he worked at that time. The workers had piled up the tiles and were going to crush them as unwanted garbage. The tiles were very beautiful, with round flares and ornaments on them. Dad asked the workers if he could have some of them, and they said, "Be our guest!"

Dad called Mom to ask which color she would prefer: pink, pale green, or chocolate brown. She chose the latter. The tiles arrived in Tbilisi in boxes and later adorned a beautiful custom-built fireplace in the corner of the study, complete with a white granite mantel top. In my mind's eye, it is always spring, and the blue vase—my parents' wedding present—is full of lilies of the valley. Mom sits on the couch reading, and Dad is at his table writing. I keep them there for a while and then quietly close the door.

I know Dad would be very proud of the way his children's lives turned out. That little boy running after his grandfather not to be lost in the woods—look at your family now! Thank you!

Seven

VACATIONS

My fondest memories are connected with our winter trips to Bakuriani, a ski resort in Borjomi Gorge. Soviet schoolchildren did not get Christmas holidays. They got winter break around the New Year, starting at the end of December on the 29th or 30th and ending on January 11. Mom would take an annual leave to take us to Bakuriani.

We would leave on New Year's Day, as the day was less traveled and trains were less crowded. We would take a train from Tbilisi to Borjomi, a town with famous mineral springs and a spa in the south of Georgia. In Borjomi, we would change trains to board a smaller train which ran between Borjomi and Bakuriani on a narrow single-track line.

The seats were not numbered, and we had to board the train fast in order to get a seat. When I was very little, I remember how I grabbed Mom's hand; I was afraid of getting lost in the crowd, as everybody was elbowing their way to get to the steps and claim seats. Some had lots of luggage. People carried skis and sleds as well as bags and suitcases, and you had to avoid getting hit by these items as well.

In those days, we rented an apartment in a house that only had an outhouse. So, for kids' nightly needs, we had to carry a potty in a special black canvas bag. I was trusted to carry it. That was my luggage. I hated if I hit the bag against something, because the lid would make a sound against the potty, which mortified me. I thought the sound would give away the contents. Fortunately, we stopped carrying it when we grew up.

The train signal sounded like a cuckoo's call, and that is why everybody called the train *Cuckooshka*, a Russian word for a cuckoo.

For some reason, the Russian word sounded more befitting of the multinational crowd travelling to Bakuriani than a Georgian word for a cuckoo, and the name stuck. For many years, the train was pulled by a steam locomotive. It ran along the monorail winding up through the mountains. Fuel and water supplies would run out fast going uphill, and the train would make long stops at some stations to get refueled and get more water.

There were iron stoves in the corner of each car, which the ticket conductor would attend to. Sometimes young people would jump off the train and take shortcuts in the woods, daring one another to meet the train at the next stop. It was a challenge but also not a very risky one, as the train crawled slowly anyway.

The way to Bakuriani was like a picturesque scene from a fairy tale. The woods in Borjomi Gorge have mainly evergreen trees, like fir and pine. Snow-covered fir trees looked very beautiful indeed, almost regal and majestic. Every time we travelled from Tbilisi—where there was no snow and maybe none was expected that winter—I admired the snow I saw from the window of the train. Later, when I read Robert Frost's poetry on snow, I thought he must have written about those woods of my childhood. Mine were the same deep woods, and even crows sounded the same way as in some of the poems, disturbing the silence.

Snow was everywhere, and you could tell which snow had fallen recently—it looked fluffy and pure. I liked to look out of the window thinking of snow. Occasionally, I could see little marks on the snow made by some animal or bird.

Inside the train was another story. Adults and children, all finally seated, would start getting to know one another. Most often, they would find acquaintances and friends. If they didn't know one another before the journey, by the time the train reached Bakuriani, they would be best friends indeed.

Usually by the time we were seated, we were ready to eat. Mom would give us boiled eggs, *khachapuri*, chicken, and cookies—all cooked and baked beforehand especially for the train ride. I loved eating on the train and watching the scenery outside. Since it was New Year's Day, people exchanged candy, with wishes for a sweet new year and sweet old age. According to the Georgian tradition, you don't have to know people to give them candy on New Year's Day. It is a tradition that everyone usually carries sweets and exchanges them, saying, "May you age as sweetly as this candy." Naturally, there was a lot of candy exchanged.

Somebody would usually have a guitar and sing or tell jokes and make everybody laugh. Games were very popular, and everybody was welcome to participate—the more the merrier. By the time the train reached Bakuriani, lifelong friendships had been forged. That journey itself was a lot of fun. Later, the steam engine locomotive was replaced by an electric train. Our favorite *Cuckooshka* was retired and put on a pedestal in the Borjomi Train Station. It stands there as a sweet reminder of happy winter journeys for so many people.

Arriving in Bakuriani gave me a special thrill as soon as I breathed in the pure, cold, crisp air. I anticipated fun and excitement during the day as well as warm evenings in our landlord's house. The house we usually stayed in was at the edge of the woods. It was a big two-story log cabin that the landlord built himself. Ours was a very cozy room which got heat from an iron stove. There were stoves in all the rooms of the house, with neat piles of wood next to them. Mom was very good at making up the fire, but usually it was our landlord or landlady who lit it for us.

There were little strips of pine wood that were used for starting a fire. I loved smelling them, as they had such a sweet fragrance. Even the fire gave off that smell. In the evening, Mom would cook on the stove. Sometimes we baked potatoes with the skin on in one of the stove compartments. We enjoyed those potatoes. I just loved sitting in front of the stove and looking into the fire through a little opening in the stove door.

Everything about the Bakuriani of my early childhood was exceptional and unique. We read books in the evening while sitting close to the stove and occasionally throwing more wood into it. We played games with our landlord's sons or other tenants. Sometimes we went for a walk before going to sleep.

Nights in Bakuriani were very cold, as with the sunset, frost would set in. I have never seen such shiny green stars against a very black sky as I saw there. Our beds were very warm, as we had thick woolen eiderdowns that our landlady made herself from the wool of their own sheep. So during the night, when the fire died, we felt quite comfortable. In the mornings, our landlady would come in and light the fire for us before we got up. On our later visits to Bakuriani, we started staying in the resorts, and we missed the rustic flavor that gave our early childhood experiences in Bakuriani a special distinctiveness.

I was very little when I first tried skiing, and I fell in love with it. I started cross-country skiing at first. There was a beautiful field called Ia Gora's Field. I don't think anybody knew the etymology, even if there was one. The field was situated deep in the woods, and you had to follow ski trails left by other skiers. The field itself would appear suddenly as a surprise, a bright spot, a white vastness, always sunny and promising.

That was the thing with Bakuriani: no matter how much snow would fall overnight, the next day the sky would be bright blue, with bright sun and not a single cloud. There were other days when it snowed and didn't seem to let off, which made us all anxious, as it was harder to ski when it snowed so much. Our landlady taught us to watch the smoke coming out of the neighbor's chimney. If the smoke went straight upward into the sky, it was a sign of a bright day in the morning. If it curled sideways, broke, and trailed down, it would snow.

We tested the sign over the years and had to agree with our landlady. We were always on the lookout for upright smoke. Our landlady also showed us how to rub animal fat that she kept in a jar on our leather snow boots to make them waterproof.

I was in second grade when some parents decided to organize a cross-country competition on Ia Gora's Field. There were lots of kids who wished to participate, including Gogi and I. We were given numbers to put on our jackets. When one of the parents gave a signal, we all glided out. Well, some did, and some faltered or fell. It was great fun. I won third and was very proud of it. Gogi, however, didn't place, and I rubbed it in for quite some time.

As I grew older, I decided I liked alpine skiing better. So I switched to that and later fell in love with slalom and stayed with it all my life. It took me a couple of seasons to master it, but I managed to learn it well.

We went to Bakuriani every winter and I discovered that skiing is one of those skills you never forget. Local farmers also offered rides on sleighs. Actually, horses with blinders pulling sleighs was the preferred means of transportation there.

I was in middle school when I first saw *Sun Valley Serenade*, an American wartime movie very popular in the Soviet Union and often shown in movie theaters long after the war was over. It was well-liked by postwar generations of moviegoers in Georgia, not just because of Glenn Miller's band and the great music but because of its spirit and general feel. As it was so popular, it never lost its charm, and the movie theaters often ran it.

After the film came out, there appeared many sweaters vaguely resembling those that John Payne wore. In Georgia, these sweaters were all the rage. Every self-respecting young man had to wear one. They were usually homemade by creative women who knitted well. Those who were more daring and imaginative even cut off brims from men's felt hats, leaving a small piece of brim to create a peak. The overall look was that of a cap worn in the movie.

For me, the movie was all about the figure skater Sonja Henie, a multiple-time Olympic, world, and European champion. In the movie, she also skied fabulously. She inspired me to excel in downhill and slalom. Once I even tried to ski, just like in the movie, between the legs of an unsuspected guy I did not even know. The guy was resting on his ski poles on a slope with his legs spread out. So I attempted to ski between his legs as unexpectedly and skillfully (or so I hoped) as it was in the movie. I was not Sonja Henie, though, and we both tumbled into the snow and rolled down the slope.

The guy had glasses on, which fell in the snow, and he had to squint and look for them. He kept cleaning them, all the time repeating, "Couldn't you see me standing there? Why did you bump into me?"

I was too embarrassed to explain what I'd had in mind. I just got up, shook off the snow, and skied downhill as gracefully as I could manage at that moment, coming to a full stop at the bottom with a sharp turn that caused snow to drift, which I always enjoyed. I knew it looked good. I hoped to show him, in case he was watching, that I could ski. I knew how to make turns, not bump into obstacles, and stop. In other words, I was not a complete klutz.

I experienced my first earthquake in Bakuriani one winter. It was a gray, overcast day. I stood with a group of skiing buddies resting on the slope and chatting. And just because I was standing at that moment and not skiing, I suddenly felt a slight jolt, immediately followed by another one more powerful and lasting. The earth swayed and shook under my feet.

It all happened suddenly and was over very soon. I remember some eerie feeling and the sound of a muffled clap and crunch, as if the woods were groaning. The trees shook, and some dry branches cracked and fell down in rapid succession. A woman in the distance started to call her kids: "Come inside! There is an earthquake!"

We all laughed at her ignorance. Somebody even called out, "Don't listen to her! You are better off here!" I don't remember what it was on the Richter scale, but some old buildings got serious cracks. Luckily, nobody was hurt.

What stays with me from the Bakuriani of my childhood are the woods, ski slopes, and rooftops covered with snow. There are fir trees standing majestically in their royal presence, a woodpecker working diligently somewhere not far away, a dog barking at passing horses—all the country sounds. In some spots, tiny snow crystals sparkle in the bright sunshine. That sunshine too is from my childhood. It lights up the snow, and from the snow reflects back into the sky. Everything on the slopes and in the meadows stays pure and untouched.

The fun and laughter and all the noise of the carefree childhood winters carry across the years. They linger and cling to my memory like a lost snowflake frozen to the windowpane, afraid to be swept away.

Kvishkheti is a beautiful village in central Georgia. We would go there for the whole season during our summer vacations. We stopped going there when we built our own country house in Mtskheta, near Tbilisi.

Tucked at the foot of the mountains, Kvishkheti had a very

agreeable climate and was a popular vacation spot for city dwellers. There was the Writers' House, a typical Soviet rest home for members of the writers' union. We spent a memorable summer there once. Otherwise, we usually rented apartments inside the homes of the local farmers.

We played with local kids and other kids from Tbilisi who were vacationing in Kvishkheti like us. One summer day stays with me forever for the incident I had there. I was probably ten or eleven. We were renting an apartment in a farmer's home. They had a big dog who was quite smart but not overly friendly. The landlord would take him hunting sometimes.

One day, the dog was having his evening meal in the yard, and some of the food fell out from his bowl. Trying to be helpful, I pushed the fallen piece closer to his bowl. Just that same second, I felt a fierce bite on my shin. I jumped back. It hurt, and I got suddenly very scared.

As luck would have it, Dad saw everything from the balcony. He immediately came downstairs and took me to the nearest hospital. They cleaned the bitten area. It turned out that the dog had just grabbed my leg and broke my skin but did not reach the bone, as the bite was not very deep. They immediately gave me one dose of rabies vaccine. Dad took the rest of the medication with him and gave it to me as instructed.

Thankfully, he didn't have to give me shots every day. It was a very painful shot into the tummy. I had to endure the treatment for the promise to have some special dessert or to go to the village clubhouse to see a movie in the evening.

The Kvishkheti village clubhouse was an institution in itself. Like any village clubhouse or community center, it was a meeting place where young people gathered for fun and amusement. Movie screenings were usually accompanied by loud comments, catcalls, shouts, and jeers. If the movie was in Russian, some additional explanation or translation was needed, and that created a distraction but also additional entertainment. Usually there was a wise guy who would crack jokes loud enough for everybody to hear and make the whole evening even more amusing and hilarious.

Since Gogi was born in August, he never had a birthday party in Tbilisi, unlike Revaz or me. So, for his party, he would usually invite kids that we met in the summer. Sometimes the same kids would go to the same resort year after year, and if we happened to all be together at the same place, it seemed like inviting old friends.

His birthdays always had an added bonus in Kvishkheti. Our grandparents, Bebe and Babu, would arrive to celebrate with us. Kvishkheti was not very far from Tbilisi. If they took the morning train, they would usually be there by lunchtime. We looked forward to their arrival and counted the hours and minutes. They always brought our favorite treats and presents—and most importantly, they brought themselves.

We had Babu, as our very own guide, tell us about some historic battles that took place in that region at the beginning of the seventeenth century. There is a village, Tashiskari, right next to Kvishkheti. It is famous for its sulfur baths, and we would sometimes go to bathe. The village has a special historical significance, since it is the place where the Georgian army prevailed over a legion from the Ottoman Empire in 1609.

The story has it that Giorgi Saakadze, the military commander of the Georgian army, had a feast to commemorate the victory at the very spot we visited, right there under the huge oak tree. The tree was so wide that it took several men to enclasp it. We listened mesmerized by Babu's stories as we imagined those events so far away and yet so tangible.

There was an ancient watchtower on the top of one of the hills in Kvishkheti. It had a round shape and was built out of stone, with gun ports. Georgia, which was constantly under attack all throughout her history, is studded with such watchtowers. The towers were used not necessarily to repel attacks from enemy forces but to send signals about the approaching threat. That was an established way of messaging in ancient Georgia: lighting fires and signaling from one tower to another.

Going to the Black Sea coast for our summer vacations was always a treat. When we got closer to the sea, I would become restless with anticipation, as the air would gradually change its aroma to smell more of sea water, salt, fish, and hot pebbles. Closer to the water, certain sounds would become more prominent—waves hitting against the shore, callings of seagulls, children shouting. The usual combination of nautical fragrances and noises promised the glee, cheerfulness, and new adventures so indispensable to vacation spots.

We used to go to the Abkhazia coast of Georgia, as the climate was drier there, unlike the southern beaches. We spent several summers in Gagra, Gudauti, and Bichvinta. All of them are now in the area so shamelessly occupied by Russia and inaccessible. Most of the once beautiful places are now dilapidated and in disrepair.

We would leave early in the morning, with us kids sitting in the back and Dad and Mom in front. It was a long way to get to the West Coast. We would usually stop overnight at my aunt's apartment in Kutaisi. Aunt Mariam, or Tsutsa as she was known to family and friends, was Dad's younger sister and lived in Kutaisi, the second largest city in Georgia. She was also a medical doctor, married to an engineer who worked at an automobile plant there. They had two children almost the same age as me and Gogi. I loved those visits, as I loved to be with my relatives.

The following morning, we would be on the road again heading to the sea. Journeys to the seaside were always enjoyable. In some places, the highway passed through beautiful villages, and I loved to observe the village life that would flash by, alternating with memorable scenic views. Sometimes Dad would stop the car, and we would pile out to look at gorgeous views. In many places on the motorway, mountains were drilled to create tunnels. I loved when the winding road took us high up onto the mountain and then entered one tunnel after another as it headed down again to follow the coastline. Sometimes the road would slope fast and create stomach-flipping and ear-plugging moments.

Once, we listened to Voice of America in our car. Somebody was flipping through the channels, and suddenly we heard a gentleman speaking Georgian in a slightly stiff manner. He talked about the arms race and human rights and some such things that I didn't much understand and didn't care about—but then he said his name and that we were listening to the Georgian service of Voice of America from

Washington, DC. What was amazing was that the voice carried very clearly without any channel interference.

Listening to "enemy" radio stations was strictly forbidden. The Soviet government, being on the lookout for the Soviet citizens' moral character, made it their mission to save citizens from "capitalist lies and propaganda." All the foreign radio stations usually had static, and it was difficult to hear what was being said. However, people listened even through static and paid attention.

I remember how I once listened to a horrifying account of people trying to escape from East Berlin into West Berlin catapulting their children over the wall. I remember those accounts more than anything else, because it was about children and parents, and I wondered what it would be like to become so desperate as to catapult a child away in hope of a better life in the unknown.

The fact that the voice carried so effortlessly while we were on our way to the Black Sea that day could be explained by the proximity to the sea and open space. Or maybe because we were traveling up the mountain, the interference was less effective, as we were away from the control towers. Many years later, I was able to put a face to the name when I met the gentlemen from VOA in Washington, DC. I was one of the many thousands he had been broadcasting to over the years.

Most of the Black Sea coast had pebble beaches. The pebbles shone beautifully in the sun after the water washed over them. The only drawback was that it was hard to walk on them barefoot.

I loved collecting pebbles. I have some here in a jar brought over as part of Georgia. I also have a pebble in the shape of a heart, and it has a hole in the middle. This one is a memento from the small town of Bichvinta.

Not all of the Black Sea coast has pebbles. There is a little town, Ureki, where one can see sand instead of pebbles. The sand there is special. It has tiny magnetic particles that make the sand the color of steel. There is magnetic sand all along the Ureki coast. When the sun warms up the sand, it enhances the sand's medicinal power. People who suffer from arthritis as well as some bone disorders are known to enjoy the sand's curative qualities.

We went there only once when we visited Mom's cousin and her family who live there. The sand was indeed something special, and the shore was so shallow one could walk for at least a thousand feet into the sea with the water reaching up to the waistline.

One summer, we were at the Black Sea coast in Bichvinta. The name of the town comes from the Georgian word *pichvi*, meaning pine. Indeed, there are gorgeous pine trees all along the coast there. This once-beautiful town is located in the Abkhazia territory and, like so many others in that area, is controlled by Russia today.

I was starting fifth grade that fall, and the summer was memorable for many reasons. We rented rooms in a house very close to the water. Because it was so close, Gogi and I were allowed to walk over to the sea before Mom and Dad joined us. Revaz was very young then, and Mom didn't spend much time on the beach. I didn't swim, but I loved playing at the water's edge. That day, I played with other kids. Somebody brought a big inflatable raft, and I climbed on it. The raft floated farther and farther from the shore with me on it. I enjoyed the ride, looking up at the sky and watching the clouds.

A little boy, the owner of the raft, swam up to me and kicked the raft from underneath. I fell into the sea and panicked, as I did not know how to swim. I was far from the shore. I kicked my hands and feet for a couple of minutes but could not stay on the surface any longer. There were lots of people all happily swimming or playing in the water around me, but nobody could hear my cries for help.

When I started to go to the bottom, my instinct told me to kick the bottom with my feet as hard as I could and go up to the surface to get some air. I would gulp air and be pulled back down. Then I would kick the bottom, pop up, and then down again, maybe four or five times. It must have been more than that. I was desperate, scared, and frantic.

When I popped up one more time, I saw Dad had come to the beach and start taking off his prosthesis. Just then, he saw me, and he stared in horror, fumbling with the straps of the prosthesis. I could sense he was horrified, afraid for me, and angry that I went that far. What was I thinking? All these thoughts flashed by in my head and were gone, as

I was already tiring out. Luckily, right then, somebody grabbed me and started dragging me to shore. Apparently Gogi had seen me struggling in the water and called one of the bigger guys to save me.

I had a lot of the Black Sea water in me. That evening, I ran a fever of 39 degrees C. That was it. I did not go into the water that summer if Dad was not there. He tried to teach me to swim, but every time the water reached my throat, I panicked and asked him to stop teaching me. That fear of water has stayed with me all my life.

There was a celebrity sharing the rented house with us that summer: composer Revaz Lagidze. He was the author of symphonies, movie soundtracks, and popular songs. His song "Tbiliso" had made him especially famous, and I remember when he was out in the street, people would recognize him and start singing the song to express their love and appreciation. The song is still timeless and the best modern song about Tbilisi.

That summer, I met his daughter, who was younger than I was, but we still played together. Later, her dad would write an opera and name it after her, *Lela*. He was a humble man, jovial and sociable.

That summer, I also met two young men from Sri Lanka. Back then, it was called Ceylon. They appeared one day on the beach and stood out from the crowd because they were fully dressed and even wore ties. They must have been to a meeting or something and then strolled to the beach.

Dad liked to show off how well we could converse in English. Gogi was reluctant to comply and didn't even come close, but I was eager to meet these people and struck up a conversation. They were touring the USSR and were visiting Georgia as part of their business trip. They asked me about my school and family, and we talked for a while. Dad stood in the background and beamed with pride.

Later that winter, we received a letter from Ceylon. I am still surprised that the letter reached us. I don't remember much of the content, but I have memorized the sentence in the P.S. at the bottom: "Nana, you speak English very well. Keep it up." It was indeed an encouragement for a fifth grader.

Eight

MTSKHETA

Often in the mornings between deep sleep and awakening, before I open my eyes, I clench at the tail end of a dream before it completely melts away in a blur and leaves me thinking and remembering. It is the feeling of content and comfort that lingers above the images that quickly slip away. It is something warm and ultimately kind and good and happy. It is so good that it pains me to let it go. That is when I know I dreamed of Mtskheta. My heart aches with longing and fondness. It is all inside me and yet so far away in distance and time. It is the familiar comfort of the homestead.

I was maybe twelve years old when my parents started thinking about acquiring a country house. They wanted a place close to Tbilisi, so that Dad could get to the clinic fast in case of an emergency, and yet far enough away to feel like the country. For several months, the whole family would get into our car and drive around the countryside looking for possible house properties.

One other requirement that both Mom and Dad had apart from location was running water. Many places around Tbilisi did not have it. People had water tanks to stock up on water and used it sparingly. My parents could not have that. It was because of the lack of running water that they had to pass on some charming places that were otherwise very appealing.

Then one day, they were taken to Mtskheta, the ancient capital of Georgia, thirty kilometers from Tbilisi. The property was in a place called Narekvavi, one of the suburbs of Mtskheta. There was a one-story unfinished building on a large plot. Most importantly, there was running water. This made it a winner.

Dad's close friend Shota Janelidze was an engineer and introduced Dad to an architect, Otar Kalandarishvili. Mr. Kalandarishvili was the lead architect of the hotel Iveria, which was being built in downtown Tbilisi at that time. He had recently returned from a trip to the United States (I think it was California that he visited) and was full of ideas. My parents wanted a contemporary building, and Mr. Kalandarishvili was only too happy to design a contemporary country house.

I remember the discussions he had with my parents. He would spread the blueprint with a beautiful drawing of a building on the table and point out the features. Mom and Dad wanted a flat roof and plenty of open space inside. This was exactly what the drawing showed. In the course of discussions, the design underwent several modifications. Eventually, after Mom and Dad approved the design, the construction started.

I was fascinated by the whole process. It was a very challenging undertaking for many reasons. They decided to leave the existing building. It would serve as the ground floor, and the second floor would be built on top of it. The ground floor did not have a high ceiling, but the new design would compensate for that by making the second floor spacious and airy. It was going to be a brick house with French windows, a very wide veranda in front, narrower on the side, and a flat roof.

Building materials were not readily available, and there was a very limited number of stores that would sell them. So when Dad set out to fulfill his dream, he used networking and handy connections. The trunk of his car was always full of samples of wood, building blocks, and bricks. I remember one day, he brought some bricks to show Mom, as they had to decide on the type and color. They chose bright red bricks.

Dad's summer vacations were entirely overtaken by overseeing the construction. He found laborers among the men in the neighboring village. They would arrive on a bus, and at the end of the day, if it was too late, Dad drove them home. He was as helpful as he could be. He sometimes would drive to a nearby restaurant to bring hot meals for the construction workers for lunch. Other times, Mom cooked for them.

I loved to watch the masonry work. It required dexterity to scoop mortar mix, spread it on a finished line of bricks, put a brick on the mortar spread, and remove excess mortar to use it on the next brick. There was something satisfying in watching the formation of accurate lines of bricks. The construction workers used a level to check horizontal surfaces and a plumb-bob to check the vertical lines of bricks. I learned how to prepare mortar mix as well as how to apply it. I even tried to lay one or two bricks myself as accurately as I could. I remember which wall of the house has my bricks in it.

In fact, I think I was merely tolerated as a curious girl who meddled more than she helped. Gogi, on the other hand, was assigned more serious tasks. That summer, we had one of Dad's relatives staying with us. He was an accountant and was very critical that Dad did not keep a ledger to conduct the business. According to him, it was unacceptable that there was no accounting and reporting of daily activities.

So he taught Dad how to keep records. He created the first sample page in a notebook. He wrote names of the laborers, days and hours they worked, and how much they were paid. At the bottom of the page, the meticulous record-keeper also wrote: "Two free laborers: 1. Batoni Beno, 2. Gogi." My grandpa was an eager laborer when he was around.

I remember those happy days when everybody was busy from early morning to sundown. There was a clear vision of a house that we were creating with our own hands, and we couldn't wait to see the finished result. The house of my parents' dreams was shaping up into a solid beauty of brick and glass. There was an immense satisfaction in knowing that we had taken part in its creation.

It was that first summer when we set about the construction that I started to believe in life's strangest twists and surprises. Over the first several weeks, our neighbors stopped by to welcome us to the neighborhood. They were always curious to know what we planned to build there. Some would stay to give advice; explain about the soil, climate, and advantages or disadvantages of cultivating grapes; or share their own gardening experiences.

The bottom end of one of the gardens faced our plot across the street. It was more of a cornfield than a garden, as there were not many trees there but mainly corn. It was enclosed by a mesh wire fence.

One day, an old man stood at the fence and greeted us as we were all scattered in our yard. This was followed by an exchange of usual pleasantries and thank-yous. I could feel Dad tense up, but he kept his cool and did not show any emotions.

"Are you any relation to Pirran Bochorishvili?" asked the old man.

"Yes. I am his grandson," said Dad.

"I thought so. I knew your grandfather."

Well, I thought Dad had also recognized the man, and even though he did not show it, he was not happy to find this person in such close proximity to our new house. When we had said goodbye and returned to our house, Dad told Mom, "I could recognize that voice anywhere, anytime. That is one of the NKVD men who came late one night to our house to arrest Levan. I was only fifteen then, but I remember everything very vividly."

Levan, Dad's uncle and Pirran and Ivlita's only remaining son, continued to be hostile toward Soviet rule and was a member of one of the underground organizations. It was in 1926 when the NKVD finally came for him.

"Pirran, we came for your son Levan. Is he at home?"

Levan was taken to Tbilisi and then sent to Solovki, one of the most notorious and vicious of the Soviet prison camps, located on the Solovetsky islands, an archipelago in the White Sea, Russia. Then he was sent to Siberia. He was imprisoned until 1932, and then he was imprisoned again in 1937, this time as a Trotskyist. Pirran and Dad went to see him in prison in Tbilisi before they sent him away. Dad had a neatly folded ten-ruble bill with him and wanted to pass the money to Levan, but when he took the bill out, it fell to the ground. Fortunately, another prisoner saw it, winked at Dad, and stepped on it before the guard saw what had happened.

That was the last time they saw Levan. There was a verbiage during the purges that "the prisoner was transported incommunicado." This was an unfortunate euphemism and often meant that the prisoner was executed. However, families wanted to believe that their loved ones were indeed sent away into prison labor camps and could not correspond. To be in denial helped the families cope with what was left of their lives.

When World War II started, there was a surge of hope, as it was rumored that the prisoners were released to fight the Germans. It was true. However, the "political prisoners" formed "penalty battalions." They were stationed in front of the Red Army formations and were used as a shield to protect the army. The lucky ones might have ended up as POWs and never returned to the Soviet Union. My grandmother Nadya always hoped that Levan was somewhere abroad.

And here was Dad so many years later with his family, happily constructing a country house, and encountering a past which in reality had never left him. Luckily, the old man's house itself was on another street; it was his cornfield that backed our street. Once he called Gogi and me and offered corn that he had in his hands. We had to be polite and take it. We thanked him but later avoided him. We soon fenced our own yard and did not see his field at all. Not long after that, the man sold his field, and the new neighbors built a house there.

One summer, my parents decided to take a break from construction activities and relax for a week or so. We all went to the seaside. My grandpa and Iza, my dad's cousin, stayed behind to oversee the work, which was still underway. By that time, the second floor of the house was already finished and roofed, but there was a lot of work still to be done. The second floor still didn't have doors and windows. The staircase was not finished yet, and a big wooden plank was propped against the balcony from the yard. We used it to reach the second floor. The yard didn't have a fence yet.

Iza stayed there all by herself one night. To ward off any potential intruders, she kept talking loudly to herself, pretending that she was in communication with people inside the house.

"Yes, Gogi, I am coming. Just give me a second."

"No, I will bring it myself."

Then, when she eventually went to sleep quite early, she was suddenly jolted awake by a banging sound. Somebody was coming up the plank. Iza jumped out of bed and saw a stray cow that must have lost its way in the dark and clomped up the plank directly to the second floor.

Mom and Dad wanted a staircase of solid oak, but they did not trust just anybody to build it. Dad hired the artisan who had previously built the shelves in his study in Tbilisi. The architect also designed the staircase. Each step was meticulously measured to fit correctly. When it was finally finished, the staircase was a magnificent creation.

Dad's friends from his hometown of Tkibuli sent him doors and window frames based on the specifications that he had requested. They also sent wood for flooring. The lumber was accompanied by a carpenter whom Dad had hired. He stayed in our house for the duration of his work.

We were allowed to choose our own rooms. I chose the room opening onto the balcony in the front of the house, far away from the entrance. I thought it was the best room in the house. An open staircase next to my room led to the flat roof. The house overlooked the Aragvi river gorge and mountains.

The architect had designed an awning in one of the corners of the roof. It was of a light construction with a brick wall and two iron poles joined at the top and spaced out at the bottom, creating a rectangular support in the front center of the awning's flat roof. When the awning was finished, it looked cool and unusual, and it became my favorite spot in the house, especially in the evenings if I needed some breeze and quiet time. It was a secluded place to unwind at the end of a hot day.

When the house was finally finished, it looked very beautiful. It was all red brick, with French windows and a wraparound veranda with a marble floor on two sides of the house. The much wider part was on the front, and the narrower part was on the side. When it was newly built, there were not many trees in front of it, and it was easily visible from the road. We had visitors stopping by and asking to be allowed to have a closer look at it. It was really unusual—very modern and light, a great summer house.

Then somebody advised Dad to cover the brick walls, as they were exposed to the elements and the sun and the wind could damage the surface. So they used stucco to cover Dad's handpicked red bricks.

The house was situated on quite a large piece of land, which consisted of an upper yard adjacent to the house and a garden on a lower piece of land with an orchard. This was where Mom started a vegetable garden. She had beds of cilantro, basil, parsley, carrots, and rows of tomatoes and cucumbers. At one of the lower corners, they built a tiny brick henhouse. We had chickens that laid eggs for us every day. Picking up warm eggs in the morning was my favorite task.

There were some peach trees and a big almond tree that came with the house. Dad planted apple trees and Mom's favorite, fig trees. I have never eaten tastier figs than the ones we had in Mtskheta. We also planted additional peach trees, which were Mom's other favorites, and also white and red cherry trees, as well as sour cherry, persimmon, and pear trees.

Mom and Dad always liked silver fir trees and planted them in the upper part of the yard. With time, the little fir trees grew tall in their silvery splendor and provided comforting shade. We soon discovered that it was not just Mom and Dad who loved them. The visiting birds found them especially appealing. A couple of blackbirds sang their love songs in the evenings and early mornings, sitting in the furry branches and enjoying our garden.

One spring, somebody brought us sour plum trees from West Georgia, which we planted in the lower garden. The trees bore sour plums called *tkemali*. When the plums got ripe, we would gather them in baskets. Revaz would climb the tree, as those on the top were not to be missed either.

Then we would start the ritual of cooking the sour sauce of the same name. The plums had to be washed and put to boil in a big bowl. Herbs, spices, and garlic were to be added later and simmer in the thick bubbling sauce. The aroma of cooking tkemali would fill the kitchen and the yard. The making of tkemali sauce was something we looked forward to, as Mom and Grandma teamed up to cook this wonderful creation. We were there to help them wash the herbs, crush coriander and garlic, and prepare the bottles for the sauce.

One year, they brought shoots of concord vine from Guria in West Georgia. With time, the vine shoots made their way up the balcony, winding around the rails and creating a flavored shade. The branches were studded with dark magenta grapes, which were very sweet and aromatic. As time went on and the grapes multiplied, Revaz started making his own wine.

Over time, Revaz, who had a green thumb, took charge of the entire garden. He worked out when to prune, plant, or harvest. Mom spent her final days in Mtskheta, and Revaz appointed himself her personal physician. In between checking on the IV drip or administering a medicine, he would run outside and tend to the garden. The garden saved him from showing his stress and frustration. It provided him with much-needed relief.

Spring exploded in colors and flavors. With so many trees, it was only natural that the ones in bloom presented themselves in their best outfits. There was a sequence to flowering. The big almond tree at the bottom of the garden would open the season, majestically spreading out branches to welcome the sun, and burst out in light pink flowers. The apricot tree standing nearby would modestly show its beautiful flowers of pure white petals with pink hearts and wait for approval from the almond tree. Sweet cherries would join in, not to be left behind, presenting their own pink flowers but of a different hue than those of the almond tree. Their cousins the sour cherries had darker pink blossoms.

Then it was time for plum trees and peach trees to stretch out, shake off the winter cold, and show off their blush pink petals. Pear trees and apple trees would complete the display with their own white blossoms. If the wind was daring enough to disturb the spruced-up trees, it would carry off the petals to dance in a spring wonderland.

We planted walnut trees and hazelnut bushes. The walnut trees bore lots of walnuts, which we gathered in early fall. Walnuts are usually shaken down, and sometimes a thick stick is used to beat against the branches to release the nuts. We would cover the ground with a big cloth to catch the walnuts. Revaz was our walnut shaker. We gathered almonds the same way. We usually harvested a lot of almonds and walnuts.

One summer, Grandpa decided to plant pumpkins. They grew well and started to spread fast along the ground. They climbed up the pear tree, which happened to be in their way. We had a very interesting-looking pear tree that summer: it bore pumpkins along with regular pears. The pumpkins were heavy and threatened to fall. So Granddad came up with the idea of creating supports for them. He made several fixtures under the pumpkins, and Mom joked that Grandpa's pumpkins were now resting on their seats.

When the peaches and figs were ripe, they would fall to the ground. We preferred picking them directly from the tree—or if they fell, we rushed to snatch them up immediately before the ants got to them. Sometimes we ate so many peaches and figs that we didn't want to eat anything else. Sweet cherries were best eaten while perched on the branches of the tree. Those summers were the healthiest and happiest summers of all. Our garden yielded so much of everything that we shared it with our neighbors and friends in Tbilisi.

I read somewhere that putting a fruit mask on one's face was good for one's skin. So, when I crushed sour cherries or peaches or any other fruit to make juice, I would put the pulp on my face. One summer, we had lots of strawberries, and those too made a good facial mask. One day, Mom's two coworkers volunteered to gather sweet cherries for their team lunch at work and drove in from Tbilisi. When I opened the gate, two young male doctors stood there. They looked so startled they even stepped back. I completely forgot that I had strawberry smeared all over my face. I directed them to the cherry trees and went to wash my face. When I came out, one of them called down from the tree above, "You didn't have to clean up. We already got used to you."

We had a hammock in the yard. That was my best-loved reading spot. Summers were my favorite time for reading for leisure, especially if I could be swaying under the tree. I miss those lazy afternoons when time stood still and there was no noise or interference from the outside world. I lived in my own bubble that Mtskheta so generously provided.

Upon entering our property, one was immediately taken by the beauty of Revaz's beds of rosebushes. Revaz was happy to be in charge when it came to roses. He really loved taking care of them. There were different varieties: red roses, tea roses, white roses. He learned all about roses and treated them with much love, respect, and appreciation. He knew when to water them and when to prune or cut the flowers. The rosebushes in their turn rewarded him with an abundance of majestic flowers.

The house was across the road from the Aragvi River, and sometimes we went down to the river's bank. I never ventured into the river but would only dip my toes to test the cold water. I liked to sit and watch the fast current. It was a pebble bank with lots of big boulders to perch on. Once I found a black stone that had the exact shape of a pestle. I took it and kept it for years. I still have it in my kitchen here in America. It is one of my treasures from home.

One evening, Revaz took our German shepherd for a walk to the river. After a while, they rushed back, both panting and visibly shaken. Apparently, a herd of cows had claimed the bank first. When they saw our dog, they probably assumed he was a wolf. First they moved close to one another, then they lowered their heads and charged toward the "wolf." Revaz took steep shortcuts to avoid the attack, and he and our dog kept running all the way home.

Soon after the house was built, my parents bought a billiard table. Grandpa explained to me some basic rules. What I mastered best was to chalk the area between the thumb and the index finger of my left hand so that the cue could slip easily; to chalk the tip of the cue; and to arrange the balls in a triangle in the center of the table to start the game. I loved hitting the ball and watching it roll to hit the other ball that would be positioned close to the net. I actually practiced on my own, but I didn't know all the nuances of the game.

Other everlasting memories are the evenings on the veranda. After a day's work in the garden, Grandpa would wash up, change his clothes, and brush his hair. After dinner, he was ready to relax with a book or a newspaper in a sling-chair on the veranda, but we would ambush him, asking for a story. We always had many questions about different aspects of historical events, and Grandpa's perspective was usually the most valuable. We sat long into the evenings until the stars came out and then continued sitting quietly in companionable silence, reflecting on what we had learned.

One memorable evening in July, when the moon shone brightly on us, Dad looked at it in admiration and said, "Imagine! Right now, there is a man walking on it!"

I could endlessly write about Mtskheta and still not pay full tribute to this wonderful place where we, as a family, were so happy. When we had families of our own, our kids inherited the love and appreciation. Growing up, Annie and Tika were happy there. They have stories of their own of how they played with their cousins, Giorgi, Naniko and Sandro, or some kids from the neighborhood. Sometimes they tell me, "I dreamed of Mtskheta last night." I know what they mean.

Nine

SCHOOL YEARS

I was six years old when I started school. I turned seven at the end of November. I was taken to the same school near our house where Gogi was already enrolled. It was called #1 Secondary School. In the Soviet Union, schools did not have names; they were numbered instead. Before the Soviet takeover, the school was called Tbilisi Classical Gymnasium, and many prominent writers and statesmen graduated from there.

I only spent one year there. I was going into the second grade when the Ministry of Education launched a pioneer program of schools specializing in foreign languages. This meant that certain schools were going to have an intense and concentrated foreign-language curriculum. There was going to be only a handful of such schools in Tbilisi.

Luckily, the school with the concentrated English curriculum was within walking distance from my home. It was closer than the school I attended the first year. The new school was #47 Secondary School, and it was called the English School. English classes started in second grade and were offered every day in the curriculum. My parents didn't think much and transferred me to the new school. I was happy to go to a different school, as I did not like my first-grade teacher.

The new school had an impressive history and rich traditions and had undergone many changes in the past century. It had started as St. Nino College for Women. The college was founded in 1846 and was designed as a school for daughters of nobility and the high brass. After the Soviet takeover, the college underwent ideological changes. Religious classes were banned. It stayed an all-girls' school for a while but later became coed.

The school building consisted of several sections. There was a church and a chapel in the yard adjacent to the main building. During the Soviet years, the interior of the church was whitewashed and rearranged to house the school gym. We played basketball and volleyball inside the church hall where previously religious services had been held. One of the first decrees that the first president of Georgia, Zviad Gamsakhurdia, issued in 1991 was to restore the church and renew services there.

When I was transferred to the new school, I was glad to see that many kids from the previous school had transferred as well. I was happy because I was a bit anxious to be a new student among unfamiliar kids. As a matter of fact, there were so many transfers that the school authorities opened a new class just to accommodate the transfers.

The school was off to a good start and immediately became famous. It turned into some kind of a show school at once. We had frequent visitors who attended classes and checked our progress. I still remember some rhymes and songs we learned in second grade and sketches that we produced—all in English.

Over the years, we recited, danced, and sang, starting with many of the British and American nursery rhymes and folk songs, like "Hot cross buns!" and "Polly put the kettle on!" and "I wish I were a tiny bird ..." Later, it was even, "Oh, I come from Alabama with my banjo on my knee." It was in third grade when we were first invited to appear on a kids' TV show.

We studied English following a curriculum designed especially for us and learned from textbooks written for English schools in the Soviet Union. There were other English schools in another part of Tbilisi, and there were also schools with concentrated French and German. At the beginning, the plan was to teach all subjects in English. We even got a textbook for geography specially written in English. However, teaching other subjects in English was doomed to failure, as there were not enough teachers who could teach history and geography or other subjects in English. They needed to have a good command of the language. On the other hand, teachers of English were not qualified to teach other subjects.

We got really lucky with the English teachers. We had an absolutely fascinating teacher of English and American literature. We just adored her. We started English literature in the eighth grade, tackling *Beowulf* and then *The Canterbury Tales*. Luckily, both of these were abridged. It also helped that the teacher could explain difficult passages and engaged us in discussions. She was an interesting storyteller and an attentive listener herself. We trusted and respected her, and she equally trusted us.

We could talk about anything with her. We knew she treated us as adults. We could even stay after class and ask questions unrelated to our immediate curriculum. Years later, I realized how vital it was to have somebody like her in a Soviet school. We even discussed the war in Vietnam, what she thought about Stalin, and what the role of literature was in a society. She was candid and open and really wanted to prepare us for life outside the school walls.

I was very involved in the English drama society and participated in all the theater productions over the years. The most successful one was our production of *Pygmalion*, with me in the lead playing Eliza Doolittle. We didn't have props and decided to act the story out in a contemporary setting so we could get away with modern clothes and minimal set design. I borrowed somebody's old coat that had seen better days. It was short on me, and the sleeves were short, but it was perfect for Eliza's character. I also borrowed somebody else's old and scruffy shoes, which were big on me and fell off when I walked, but that was the idea, as it reinforced the image of a poor flower girl. We didn't perform the whole play, only the first and third acts. The opening night was a big success.

We participated in a competition of foreign language productions among school students. The competition was held in the Palace of Young Pioneers. One of the competing schools presented a scene from *The Merchant of Venice*. They were perfectly made up and had beautiful costumes, obviously borrowed from a professional theater company. Our group helped one another with makeup, but we couldn't do anything about the clothes, and that was okay. We were all very anxious and nervous but as my dad always said, "If you are nervous before some big event, that will help your mind to focus, and you will mobilize and concentrate."

That theory proved right during our performance. We put our hearts and souls into our acting that night. It did not even seem like acting. We somehow happened to be in Covent Garden instead of Tbilisi. It was the best performance we had ever put on, and we won. The jury was unanimous in its decision. We got a certificate of recognition. As the winners, we were invited to be on a TV program for kids, where we performed a vignette from the play. We even toured with *Pygmalion* to Tallinn, Estonia.

I was in my senior year when a group of students from a secondary school in Tallinn, also with a concentrated English curriculum, visited our school on a short exchange program. They attended some of our English classes. We took them sightseeing, to a theater, and to other places of interest.

Then, in late spring, it came time to pay them a visit. The trip to Tallinn was memorable in many ways. As we were in our final year of school, it was a final opportunity for our drama society to be together. The trip was organized by our school. We took a train to Moscow, with two nights on the train. In Moscow, we transferred to an overnight train to Tallinn. Overall, it was a long journey, but because we were all cooped up together, we had the best time for all four days we were on the train. Even our teachers who chaperoned us participated in games and fun.

Our host was the Tallinn school that had visited us earlier that year. When Estonian students had visited Tbilisi, our school had distributed them to host families, and we organized outings to show them the city. In Tallinn, we were put up in the school gym and used the shower facilities there. We were a bit surprised, but overall, we did not care much for comfort at that age anyway. I guess we looked at it as part of the fun and adventure of the trip.

It was during our visit to Tallinn that we encountered open and undisguised animosity toward the Soviet ideology. Baltic states had been incorporated into the Soviet Union immediately after World War II, and their discontent with this was obvious and understandable. Their attitude toward the imposed rule did not change with time. To us, this attitude was not so much scary as very refreshing and even encouraging.

The first thing we immediately noticed was the general reluctance to speak Russian. Since the USSR consisted of fifteen different countries loosely called republics, Russian was the language of international communication among the peoples of different nationalities, but the Estonians tried to avoid using Russian as much as they could.

The school organized some events, and of course there was our play, but other than that we were left alone to plan our leisure as best we could. We walked in the streets of old town by ourselves. When we lost our bearings and had to ask for directions, or if we happened to go into stores, we instinctively addressed people in Russian. But nobody wanted to reply in Russian. They either genuinely did not know the language or refused to speak it. Luckily, in many instances, we could switch to English. They did not have problem with English.

One day, a group of us went sightseeing on our own. We got hungry and tired after wandering the streets. It got dark and started to drizzle. We hailed a taxi and asked the driver to take us to our school—or better yet, stop at a café or a bakery closer to the school.

The driver was an Armenian gentleman and had no problem speaking Russian. He asked where we were from and what we were doing there—all the questions a tourist gets. While we were talking, we passed a big billboard with Lenin's portrait. The driver took his left hand off the steering wheel, stretched it out to the portrait, and declared with a smile, "If you are hungry, look at this guy, and you will feel better. The hunger will pass." We almost forgot that we were hungry, he cheered us up so much.

He stopped at a bakery. How glad we were to buy buns and pastries. We stood in the corner of the bakery savoring buns and cracking jokes about Lenin.

By that time, we were already well-versed in double standards. We did not have all the knowledge or understanding yet, but we had some courage of our convictions. We already knew about dissidents and forbidden books by writers who either had disappeared in purges or emigrated abroad. We knew that what was whispered or hinted at in our homes was not to be repeated outside, unless to trusted friends. There were certain subjects and aspects of life that were handled with care.

For example, I remember it was around Easter when we traveled to Tallinn and talked among ourselves about it. For Easter, all the families would dye eggs and bake Easter cakes. Some members of families, mostly grandparents, would attend Easter services. Younger generations were discouraged from going to church, and if students were seen there, they were reported to school authorities.

My earliest recollection of a church service was me standing in a big room. I was surrounded by many adult feet that stood close to me or moved around. There was beautiful chanting in the room. I was very little, and my grandmother Nadya took me with her to a service. Moving feet was all I could see at my eye level. If I craned my head and stood on tiptoes, I could also see many lit candles.

It is from those early days that I remember the smell of incense and the tinkling sound of a censer. I also remember that Nadya would occasionally light a candle and prepare a special meal at home. Then she would dip the tip of a piece of bread into a glass with wine and put it on a plate. She would cross herself and murmur, "God rest his soul." I was allowed to watch but not interfere. When I grew up, I realized that it was a memorial service for my grandfather.

People were strongly discouraged from going to church or being openly religious. If a student had a cross showing over her school uniform, she would be chastised at the school Young Communist League (Komsomol for short) meeting, her parents would be called to school, and an entry would appear in her personal record. Big religious holidays like Christmas, Palm Sunday, or Easter were heavily attended by members of Komsomol to observe who would show up. With time, though, rules became more lax. People were less scared and more willing to go to church services.

Civil authorities, on their part, had special programs to lure us away from religious temptations during religious holidays. When I was little, there were not many TV channels in the Soviet Union. There were two local and one central channel broadcasting from Moscow. Usually on Saturday nights, right before the Easter midnight service, the Georgian TV would start a program called "Illusion." They had a special TV screening of the best of French, German, Italian, Japanese, and American films, with introductions by film critics with interesting insights and discussions.

The authorities had another trick up their sleeve when it came to Easter. The Soviet government declared Easter Sunday a National Clean-Up Day. Everybody was strongly advised to participate in it. Those who were absent had to give a good reason for missing it. We went to school on Easter Sunday morning and washed the walls and windows in our classrooms. We cleaned the yard and hallways as well. The sad reality was that we all knew why we were there and why we were doing this, but nobody could dare say or do anything about it.

Ideological education started very early. When I was in kindergarten at the age of five, I already knew many verses and songs about Party, Lenin, Revolution, and USSR. Ideological training became more focused and meaningful in elementary school. All the first graders became Little Octobrists, proudly wearing a pin with the image of a curly-haired baby Lenin. Third graders pledged allegiance to Lenin's ideas and were accepted into the ranks of the Young Pioneers. We wore red neckerchiefs until the eighth grade, when we became members of the Young Communist League, or Komsomol for short.

The difference between a free society and the ideology-driven Soviet system was a simple process worked out by the fathers of the USSR that guided people into submission against their will and natural inclinations. To a gullible observer, it would even seem that there was relative freedom there. Education was free. We were allowed to watch foreign movies and read books in translation—in general, to become well-rounded and erudite. Reading provided refuge and escape from the false reality. All of this, however, had to be within acceptable limits.

Yes, we read a lot, but we were not allowed to read certain authors or watch certain movies. Ever-vigilant ideology was on the lookout for unacceptable influences or unguided interpretations. We could not get English newspapers. The only newspapers that were readily available in the English language were the ones printed in the USSR, like the *Moscow News* or the British socialist daily *Morning Star.*

The structured and guided lifestyle did not allow us to learn about any negative or unpleasant occurrences within the Soviet Union, as they could affect our high Soviet morale. We were meticulously fed positive information on the achievements of the country, often presented in the contrast to the capitalist world where as we were constantly reminded "workers unjustly suffered," where there was "child labor," where there was an "unpredictable future and unstable life." Filtered and censored mass media played an important part in the brainwashing process. The Soviet people of all ages had to subscribe to daily newspapers and magazines, as everybody had to read ideologically sound publications.

It was a paradoxical situation, almost ludicrous, that the Easter midnight service was countered by foreign films produced in capitalist countries. In order to keep people away from the Church, they offered capitalist creations. That was one of the reasons many young people gladly stayed behind to watch the movies. The Soviet government knew its people. They knew that the chance to see *Amarcord, Rocco and His Brothers, The Nights of Cabiria, The Magnificent Seven, Blowup,* as well as films by Bergman, Kurosawa, and many other great directors was too much of a temptation to be missed.

The Soviet cinema market itself was full of foreign films. There were many movie theaters within walking distance from one another in downtown Tbilisi. All of them were very close to our school. Often, we would rush after classes to get to the midday showing of the latest foreign movie. If the movie was very popular, there was a long line at the ticket office. We would send somebody with our money to get in line and buy tickets before we got there.

Movies in the USSR were dubbed, not subtitled. That is why it usually took a while, sometimes a year or more, for movies to reach the Soviet audience. They had first to translate the script and dialogue and then dub them. Only songs would be subtitled. This is how we watched some of the great musicals, like *My Fair Lady, The Sound of Music,* and *The Great Caruso.*

Sometimes titles came out completely different in translation, especially if the original title contained an idiom. Translators would come up with the closest substitute or a descriptive title that would render the general idea but change the meaning. For example, *Some Like It Hot* became *There Are Only Girls in the Band*, and *Sitting Pretty* became *Got Cleverly Settled*. Charlie Chaplin was a favorite with the Soviet film industry. I think his political ideas contributed to the popularity, although he was undoubtedly a genius. I loved watching him.

Even with this freedom of foreign film distribution, not all movies made it to theaters. Some were shown only in private screenings to party bosses and moviemakers. *The Godfather* was one of them; *One Flew Over the Cuckoo's Nest* was another. Actually, the latter illustrates my point that there was a limit to what a Soviet person could read or see. Dangerous and antiestablishment movies were banned.

The Soviet movie rating system was different from that of other countries. Movies were usually *16-certificate*, which meant that movie posters always had a warning, "Not advisable for minors under sixteen." Even in those movies, some of the sex scenes or risqué dialogues were cut out. That made it difficult sometimes to follow the story with the distorted scene sequence. Some scenes seemed plucked out of context. We immediately recognized the Big Brother interference. We would say, "A scene has been cut out." It was clear that despite a certain freedom of watching foreign movies, we were still controlled and supervised.

Showing movies posed no threat to the regime, because the government had many ways to regulate our lives. Actually, movies were part of the big scheme, as no matter what we saw or how we aspired to the way of life we saw in the movies, we could not emulate that reality. Our lives were checked and directed while we were securely tucked behind the iron curtain. We were controlled and supervised, especially while we were growing up. Ideological organizations created to supervise young minds took care of that.

But kids talked, exchanged whispers, and told stories. The system was oppressive and manipulative. You either became one of them, a conformist, or became cynical, uncooperative, and rebellious. It could be a self-preservation instinct or common sense, but we started to create a parallel reality of our own. It was our own world, impenetrable and secure.

Paying lip service to the system did not seem hard. We honed our skills and excelled at double standards. This helped us to become defiant and have no fear. It was easier to keep our moral principles intact once we realized that we lived a lie and followed somebody else's orders. We refused to be brainwashed.

Coming to this realization took time. A colleague of mine once shared her experience and told me that she went to "inner immigration," and that helped her cope. I knew exactly what she meant. The majority of us were inner immigrants. Yes, we had a carefree childhood, but it was also controlled and regulated.

My dad had a typist who typed his manuscripts. I called her Aunt Ksenya. She lived near us. Dad would write in longhand and would give us his manuscripts to carry over to her house. She seemed old to me then. She must have been in her late fifties. She had a sister who was older than her, and both of them lived alone in a little apartment.

I would sometimes see her sister on a bus crossing herself every time the bus passed the monument to Lenin that stood proudly overlooking the square that carried his name. Many years later, Lenin would be dismantled, and the square would be renamed Freedom Square. Once, she whispered to me that she crossed herself against Satan. When she crossed herself, other passengers would cast a glance and look away quickly, as if caught seeing something illicit. Overtly religious manifestations were frowned upon at best. However, this was an old lady who was not a threat to the atheistic regime. I felt uncomfortable and slightly embarrassed myself.

Later, I regretted that I never had the guts to ask her what she meant then or about her life. However, there was no way we could launch into the subject of Lenin on a bus. And yet, I wondered. There was something I could not understand at that time, but it nagged my subconscious.

I realized later what it was I had sensed in the two sisters. They had class and upbringing, which made them stand out. It manifested in the way they carried themselves, the way they dressed, the way they talked. I always thought that the two sisters must have been from a good family that fell on difficult times after the Soviet takeover. Theirs was one of the thousands of distorted lives, including my own dad's family.

We managed to survive despite or because of what we had to put up with. We found ways to get along. It became our second nature to be vigilant and not trust everybody. We opened up only to close friends. We became resourceful and countered the authorities in our own crafty ways.

In high school, I spent many evenings copying poems from a friend's notebook into my own. These were poems by poets who had either emigrated or had fallen victim to the purges. These poets were not on the school curriculum, and their books had been banned. The government's opinion was that those poets had been deemed undesirable and could be a bad influence on Soviet minds. Years later, all these poets were officially rehabilitated and published during Perestroika, but I still cherished my tattered notebooks.

Resourcefulness was also revealed in something as trivial as making our own clothes. It was an unpleasant reality that good-quality clothes were hard to come by. Moscow stores were best stocked. That too had an ideological explanation. Foreign embassies were all situated in Moscow, and the city was the face of the country. Moscow had to keep up appearances as the capital city of the "prosperous paradise" the country claimed it was. So we often made our own clothes following patterns and designs in foreign magazines. The magazines were usually smuggled in or brought by somebody who had previously visited a capitalist state.

The fame of the Beatles reached the country long before their songs reached us. I still remember their black-and-white photos, furtive exchanges under desks, and whispered admirations: "That's Ringo Starr, that one's Paul McCartney ..." Songs were privately copied on magnetic tapes, shared, and cherished. "Yesterday" was a peep into a different world.

Clothes were not the only commodity relatively abundant in Moscow. As a rule, food staples—including cervelat sausage, chocolate, coffee, and much more—would as a rule end up on the black market. Moscow still carried these products. Once in a while, even caviar could be found in the stores there. The rumor had it that a Russian tourist went into a store that sold sausages in the German Democratic Republic and fainted at the sight of the abundance of different sausages there.

The Soviet population that traveled from different towns to visit Moscow, whether for business or pleasure, would rush to stores to buy desired merchandise—anything they could never buy in their own towns. Lines in Moscow stores were enormous. People would stand for hours and write numbers of their place in line on the palms of their hands to make sure nobody could cut in front of them. The numbers on the palms would run into the hundreds.

Precious time in lines was not considered wasted, as the reward of obtaining something pretty or coveted was absolutely worth it. Many newlywed couples who came to Moscow on their honeymoon spent most of the time in lines in stores. I knew a girl once who went to see a foreign movie several times because she was making a drawing of a dress she liked on an actress and wanted to make a similar one for herself. One of the esteemed occupations was a commodity expert or a stock manager who had free access to merchandise. Merchandisers were considered to have handy connections and were respected and admired.

According to the teachings of Marxism-Leninism, the country was in the phase of Developed Socialism, steadily moving toward Communism, which was the highest and the most advanced stage of development. When I was growing up, this ultimate phase predicted heaven on earth. Our second-grade teacher one day described Communism in such terms that even we could understand it. She said that during Communism, living conditions were to reach the highest level of development, with an abundance of food and prosperity in everything. She also said that there would be no difference between life in a village and a big city. She explained that the rural life would be as advanced as the urban life. Soviet people would have everything.

Many years later, a friend of mine invited me to her company's summer picnic in Virginia. It was a regular summer picnic organized by her employer. Suddenly, I heard a man behind me say to somebody in Russian, "This is Communism. No?" He was obviously referring to the abundance of free food and drinks and entertainment. I didn't linger to hear the response but walked away smiling. Spot on! That is exactly what we were promised back in the USSR.

During the arms race between America and the USSR, such innocuous household items as aluminum pots and pans became a scarcity, even sewing needles. It was rumored that they were sacrificed for the might of the Motherland. However, the main slogan remained resolutely at the top of the agenda: "Move forward to the ultimate victory of Communism!"

When I was growing up during the Cold War, one of the most popular Soviet slogans was "To catch up and overrun America!" You could see it on billboards, on walls in schools and hospitals. There were others, more obscure and equally less promising:

- "Communism is Socialism plus electrification of the whole country."
- "Lenin's actions live forever!"
- For maternity wards: "Happy babies are born under the Soviet star."

Even then they sounded like a joke.

Lenin's main slogan on Communism and electricity became questionable in the eighties. In the middle of the arms race between the USSR and the United States, the central Soviet TV channel broadcasting from Moscow instructed Soviet citizens to switch off the lights when leaving the room and to unplug all electrical devices that were not being used in order to preserve electricity.

On the seventh of November during our graduation year, we had to participate in a parade dedicated to the Great October Socialist Revolution. Actually, our principal came into the classroom and declared that if any of us missed the parade, we would not receive our high school diploma. We had to wear turquoise-colored cotton dresses, turquoise cotton stockings, and cotton gloves—red on the right hand and white on the left hand. We were given the gloves and stockings. I don't know whose imagination came up with the colors or design for the dresses, but we had to buy the material and then make the dresses ourselves following a pattern. Mom made mine for me. We practiced for days to perform correctly the most bizarre of presentations.

Eventually, during the parade, we passed the platform where members of the Georgian government stood. There were also other dignitaries and famous people there. We stopped in front of the platform, lifted the right hand with the red glove high above our heads, waved, and shouted in Russian, "Lenin lived!" Then, while holding the right arm up in the air, we lifted the left arm with the white glove on it and waved, shouting "Lenin is alive!" Then we paused and clapped both hands. "Lenin will live!" We knew we had to shout in Russian for Moscow bosses to hear our heartfelt love for Lenin and believe our dedication to his eternal cause.

Winter had started early that year, and it was bitterly cold that morning. Mom made me wear warm clothes under the cotton dress. I could hardly move, I was so bundled up. But I still managed to lift my arms to clap enthusiastically and with great vigor.

Education in the Soviet Union was supervised by the Ministry of Education in Moscow. Even though all the republics had their own Ministries of Education, the main directions were coming from the capital city of the Soviet Union. It was the Ministry of Education of the USSR that shaped curricula for the Soviet schools. One of the main goals was to create Soviet citizens who would be proud of the Soviet State and not so proud of their countries of origin.

That was why history classes were especially important for brainwashing. We were taught the history of the Soviet Union with a concentration on the history of Russia. There were very few hours allocated to the history of Georgia. The Moscow Ministry of Education conducted scheduled inspections all over the USSR. It meant that the ministry representatives would inspect schools and colleges everywhere.

Moscow oversaw and controlled the education process in all the republics, including scientific work, even approved dissertations. In true Big Brother tradition, the committee would inspect curricula, syllabi, lesson plans, progress in studies, and the academic performance of students as well as instructors. The Moscow committee would check not only the education system but all the research institutions, enterprises, and clinics. Moscow administrations were busy inspecting and surveying. However, this obnoxious intrusion understandably backfired and sometimes created resistance, even among the fervent local bosses. And yet, nobody wanted to look bad. Everybody got thoroughly prepared for inspections if they expected one.

One of the aspects of the educational system that Moscow was eager to check was how well the Russian language was taught. Even though Georgia was part of the Soviet Union, Georgian was the state language in the country. Education was conducted in Georgian. There were some Russian schools in Georgia as well for Russian-speaking citizens. However, offering Russian language in Georgian schools was compulsory.

My Russian was good, as I spent some time in St. Petersburg when I was little, and I also went to a Russian kindergarten. My favorite subjects at school were history, geography, and languages. I loved Georgian, English, American, and Russian literature, and I was good at writing essays.

One day, I was called into the principal's office. On the way there, I wondered if I had done anything wrong. The principal was both fair and demanding. She could be very strict, and we tried to be on our best behavior with her.

The principal sat at her desk. She looked up when I entered.

"I have a favor to ask of you," she started without beating around the bush.

I had no idea what was coming, and that added to my anxiety.

"There is a Moscow committee coming to our school tomorrow," she said. "I just had a phone call from the Regional Department of Education. They are going to administer a written test in Russian in our senior class. Titles of the compositions are sealed. They will reveal them at the time of the test. We only know that it will be based on the syllabus and from the material the class has already covered. I want you to take the test along with the seniors. You will go and sit in that classroom tomorrow."

At that time, I was in the ninth grade. I was not in the graduating class. I was a year younger—a junior. I stood at the door and tried not to register surprise. How could I? Thrilled at such trust, I responded to the urgency of request as best I could.

"I will ask you not to discuss this conversation with your friends," said the principal. "Tomorrow, during second period, you will take your pen and go to the classroom where the test will be administered. After the test, please return to your classroom."

At home, I told my parents what I had been asked to do.

Mom was understandably worried. "You don't know what they have already studied."

"I can always write a free composition," I replied.

In our schools, when we had written tests, teachers would write three titles on the board that we could choose from for our compositions. The first two were usually based on what we had already studied, and we had to analyze and write our thoughts—for example, "Women Characters in the Novel" or "A Theme of Friendship in the Novel." The third title was usually a free composition. However, a title was still given, like "Your Favorite Poet" or "Why Do I Like Spring?"

Even though I was usually well prepared to write essays based on the titles from the syllabus, I preferred free compositions because they offered flexibility, and I could be at liberty to let my imagination fly. The tenth-graders had recently completed Maxim Gorky's story "Mother." I had not read it, and I knew I could not write anything about it.

The next day, as I had been instructed, I went to take the test with the tenth-graders. I went to the classroom during the break and chose a seat in the third row. Some of the students looked surprised to see me there, but nobody said anything. They didn't ask why I showed up in their classroom. Their Russian teacher was in the classroom, and she acted as if I belonged there.

The door opened, and two Moscow committee members entered the room. We all stood up, as was the way to greet our elders. They walked over to the window and stood there, ready to observe. The teacher opened the sealed envelope that one of the committee members had handed to her. She took out a slip of paper and copied the titles on the board.

The first two titles were related to the story by Maxim Gorki. It did not surprise me, as I was expecting this. The third title was for a free composition: "My Favorite Book." I knew immediately that this would be the subject of my essay. We were given forty-five minutes—an academic hour in our schools. I wished I had thought beforehand about the possibility of getting this title as an option.

In the classroom, with minutes ticking away, I realized I didn't have much time to choose from my favorite books. Actually, because I was nervous, I was drawing a blank. Suddenly, I remembered a book I had read the previous summer. It was a collection of short stories written by Maxim Gorki. It was not my favorite book, but I immediately decided that writing about that book would also resonate with the general theme of the test, as the book was written by the same author. I have often wondered since then how at that age I made such a smart, targeted decision.

The book was a collection of stories called *Fairy Tales about Italy.* Stories were related to the writer's stay on Capri at the beginning of the twentieth century. It had been a while since I had read the stories, and I did not remember all the details, but I did remember the general feel. Some of the stories had made a lasting impression. I decided to write about their effect on me. I concentrated on some of the most vivid characters that stood out and stayed with me.

There was no time to write a draft first and then copy it. I decided not to hurry and take my time before committing my thoughts to paper. That is what I did, and I finished almost at the time the bell sounded. I returned to my class after the test and carried on with the rest of the day as if I had not been my friends' senior just an hour earlier.

Two days later, the principal summoned me again. This time, I didn't wonder if I had done anything wrong. I was just curious. She looked serious and yet broke into a sad smile when I entered.

"When I asked you to take the test and write a composition, I did not ask you to write better than everyone in that class."

And hello to you too, I thought. *Am I in trouble now?*

I stood at the door and just stared at her.

"What happened?" I finally managed.

"Your composition was singled out as the best among all the writings. They were so impressed that I sit now and worry if they will request your other tests or want to meet you."

"I can always get sick," I mumbled helpfully. Our relationship, despite the great scheme that we had just pulled off, did not allow this freedom of exchange, and the principal frowned.

"Let's hope nothing will come out of their interest. Go back to your classroom, please."

Indeed, nothing happened. But I worried every day while the Moscow committee was still at school. They left soon and never expressed a desire to meet with me. I knew a weight was lifted off our principal's shoulders.

I always felt that our principal had a soft spot for me even though she never showed it and was always her usual austere self with me. My instincts were right, as confirmed at the costume party my senior year.

We were the first graduating class from the English School. We were the Ministry of Education's pioneer project that proved successful. We thought of ourselves as the best. So it was only natural that we wanted our costume party to be outstanding and memorable.

The ball had to be held before our winter break at the end of December. We made our own decorations. We bought all the festive decorations we could find in stores, but there was not a large selection there. We could find paper streamers and confetti, but that was pretty much it.

We spent days making cotton chains to hang from the ceilings. We also made paper chains and buntings. Those who were good at drawing drew pictures of fairy-tale characters to hang on the walls. We decorated the whole school. We wanted to leave a lasting impression.

The most difficult part was getting fancy dress costumes. Dad and I went to the manager of the Opera House, whom Dad knew. I talked Dad into asking him for a costume for the evening. The manager was a friendly gentleman who was not surprised at our request.

"Yes, yes, I know. I had some other people with the same request already. Sure, we will be happy to help out this young lady here."
He called the cloakroom attendant and asked her to take me to the cloakroom and see what we could select there.

I chose Carmen's outfit—a long black dress, long black gloves, a big fan, even a silk red rose for the hair. I went to the hair salon to have my hair done.

We had invited students from other schools, and they also came all dressed up. All of us looked different and somehow grown-up, as most of us had costumes of famous characters and did our best to look the parts. There also were some very interesting concepts, like a girl with a costume of a snowflake made of white mesh and sparkles.

One of our classmates got first prize for her costume. It was a costume that she made herself, and her work was rightfully noted. She was Little Red Riding Hood. It was a very pretty costume complete with a white apron and a little basket.

During our dance, the principal approached me and asked me to follow her to her office. She said she wanted to play pranks on everyone and asked me to let her wear my dress while I waited in the office for ten minutes. I was five foot eight, as tall as she was. She was also very slender for her age. The dress was a good fit. We covered her head with a shawl that I had on my shoulders. With gloves and her face covered with the big fan, she almost looked like me.

She returned very soon, laughing that she could not fool them. My classmates immediately noticed her height as well as her walk. We forgot the shoes! She wore high heels, and they were much higher than the ones I wore that day. Somebody noticed her posture and walk. While nobody could dare assume that this person was our principal, they could see it was not me either. *What's wrong with Nana?* they wondered. Then I went out again as another Carmen and revealed the secret.

I often think about that night. It was indeed a night of merriment and enjoyment. We were ready to go into the world and conquer it, and yet we wanted to stay together forever in the familiar safety of childhood.

Because we had been together for ten years, we had developed a special camaraderie based on trust and understanding. Our recollections of one another stretched over to the first day when we were taken to school for the first time. Some of the kids cried. Some stayed brave. Over the years, we had learned how to study as well as goof around and have some fun along the way.

When we were in the fifth grade, one of the girls came to school wearing her older sister's black stockings. She looked very grown up. The stockings had a beautiful pattern and looked very foreign and unusual. It was something we did not see in the stores. The pair of them were bought on a black market. One of the classmates wanted to try them on, and the lucky owner agreed. They decided to exchange their stockings right there and then during the Georgian class. The cheek of it!

The first girl sat in the middle row and the second one farther from her, in the side row. The first girl rolled down the stocking from her right leg and passed it over. Since the other girl sat in another row, the stocking could not be passed without the teacher seeing it.

The second girl, meanwhile, took off her own stocking and sat waiting. When the teacher looked aside, the girls swapped their stockings—but not soon enough. The teacher saw the exchange and told them to step away from their desks. They each stood with one leg without a stocking and barefoot. Both of them were taken to the principal's office, and their parents were called to school.

Some of the teachers were very strict. Some had unreasonable demands—like our math teacher, who would only accept homework written in violet ink. If a student used blue ink, that homework would not be accepted. If a student left a notebook behind, the teacher's reaction would be, "Why did you not leave your head behind as well?"

School friends, places, and memories are intertwined in time and space. They create a vivid pattern that never fades with time. So many places are connected to my friends' homes, birthday parties, and places of entertainment. I loved going to my friends' birthday parties, but I absolutely loved my own birthday parties.

I remember weeks before my birthday, when we had to write a date in our notebooks for a classroom assignment, I always thought, *It's already one day closer to my birthday.* Mom cooked my favorite dishes, but everybody mainly ate *khachapuri* and drank lemonade. My birthday, being at the end of November, would also mark the start of tangerine and persimmon season. We always got those for my birthday dinner table. Chestnuts were in season as well, and Mom would boil them and serve them hot.

We imitated grown-ups and even appointed a toastmaster. Invariably, it was Malkhaz, a classmate of mine. He loved to toast me in an overdone platitudes that always made us laugh. Holding a glass with lemonade, standing erect and dignified, he would start ceremoniously, "With this little glass but a big heart …"

In the USSR, schools were structured in such a way that grade school, middle school, and high school were all housed in one building, which was considered one school entity. Students continued on to another level as soon as they graduated from the previous level, so they usually carried on with the same classmates with whom they started in first grade. This continuity created a special bond between students. We had enough time to get to know one another. We shared happy moments as well as consequences of mischievous behavior. A memorable incident of the latter happened when we were in seventh grade.

Our teacher of Georgian language and literature was an elderly lady. We were her last class before retirement. We really liked her, but we somehow took advantage of the fact that she was not very demanding. We did not sit quietly and did not listen to her calls for attention.

One day, we were completely out of order. We wrote notes to one another, and if she intercepted them, we wrote new ones. We talked and giggled and stayed in a parallel reality from the teacher, who stood at the board and was visibly upset. She could not take it any longer and left the classroom.

Needless to say, we were ashamed. However, the reality of what we had done hit the moment the classroom door opened and our principal walked in. She was generally very strict, but that day her expression was just thunderous. She did not have to say much. She just rubbed in what we ourselves felt: "Immature, disorderly, and troublesome."

We were directed to bring our parents to school that night at seven o'clock and explain our behavior in front of them. That was very bad news, because our parents would really be angry. And they were. Mom did not cut me any slack because I personally did not do anything bad.

Since I did not prevent others from acting badly, I was as much at fault as any one of them.

The meeting started promptly at seven. All the students were told to wait outside in the hallway while the parents were led into the teachers' lounge. One of our classmates came directly from a concert in which he had participated. He brought his violin case with him. He was quite happy that he had played well, and that cheered us up. Otherwise, we were all scared and nervous. Apart from the Georgian teacher, there was the principal, head teacher, vice principal, and all the parents. Mom was there.

After some time, we were called in. We entered the room in single file and stood at the wall with our heads bowed. We were all so ashamed, we could not look at our teachers or our parents, for that matter. I kept scrutinizing the big buttons on Mom's coat. It was especially hard to look our Georgian teacher in the eyes. She was not happy herself and obviously did not want all this.

Then one of the parents addressed her daughter: "Now Irina, tell us what happened and if you realize what you have done."

Irina would not dare deny any responsibility. We all felt responsible for the bad judgment and horrible behavior. There was no explanation for our actions that day. We could not even explain ourselves—how childish insubordination got out of hand and turned into a disaster. Why hadn't we calmed down and paid attention? Some of the more daring students volunteered to speak up and apologize. This was the worst experience, one we equally shared and which somehow united us.

Theaters and cinemas stand out prominently in the chain of recollections of where my friends and I used to go. There was an opera house and the Rustaveli Drama Theater within walking distance from our home. My very early recollection is connected to *Swan Lake*. Not knowing much about music or ballet, and not really ready for the magic unfolding right in front of me, I wondered how it was possible to be so beautiful and ethereal. Did they dance to the music or did the music evolve around them? I remember for days after the performance, I dreamed of becoming a ballerina. Then when I saw *Giselle*, I danced before a mirror in Mom's negligee as I thought it the closest gown to Giselle's outfit.

When the Rustaveli Drama Theater started producing plays in its small hall, *Chinchraka*, translated as *The Orn Wren,* took it by storm. It was a fairy tale about love between a princess and a peasant boy, and like any fairy tale, it was really about good versus evil. There were many birds and animals played by very famous theater actors. I don't remember the plot now, but what I do remember are certain scenes and expressions and the general festivity of the occasion. It was all so very funny and very entertaining as well. It conveyed a beauty that stayed with me forever.

There were several movie theaters along Rustaveli Avenue, all close to our school: Tbilisi, Spartaki, the Rustaveli Movie Theater (or Rustaveli for short), Officers' House, Chavchavadze Club, and Artists' House, which also had its own movie theater. The latter was in our immediate neighborhood. The ticket-office lady was an acquaintance of ours and always had tickets for us even when they were sold out. I saw my first Disney movies there. It was a special screening. All the movies were in black and white, but that didn't take away the magic that they carried. Oh, how we laughed that day.

The rows in movie theaters were numbered, and we knew which seats to ask for when we went to buy tickets. For example, in Officers' House, the first row of the second section was where you could slouch and stretch your legs. In Rustaveli, it was better to sit in the first rows of the orchestra to avoid being hit by a cigarette butt or sunflower shells dumped from the balcony, and because the afternoon shows were mainly attended by teenagers, chances of those occurrences were always high.

Speaking of teenagers, it was always risky to cut classes to see a movie during school hours. Some movie-theater administrators would have raids to reveal truants and call the school to have them picked up. I never experienced this, but I was told that during a movie screening, they would switch on the light briefly, pause the movie, and ask school students to please get up and follow the movie-theater administrator.

Each movie theater is associated with the movies I saw there. For instance, I remember where I saw French comedies with the absolutely fabulous Louis de Funès, listened to Mario Lanza, watched the beautiful love story *A Man and A Woman* with Anouk Aimee and Jean-Louis

Trintignant, and saw many more unforgettable movies. Once, while watching one of the comedies with Louis de Funès, *The One Man Band*, Manana, a friend of mine laughed so hard she kept kicking somebody sitting next to her, as she thought it was one of us. She later realized that it was an unknown gentleman. She was embarrassed, but he was cool about it and didn't mind. He was in stitches himself.

The Umbrellas of Cherbourg with the beautiful Catherine Deneuve, I saw in Spartaki with my classmates Lela, Lena, and Mzia. I remember our discussions afterward. *The Sound of Music, How to Steal a Million*, and my all-time favorite, *It's a Mad, Mad, Mad World*, I saw on the Rustaveli balcony.

All the movie theaters have since been repurposed or completely destroyed. Only Rustaveli remains in its original capacity. It has been spruced up and refurbished. They sell popcorn, and there is no need to eat sunflower seeds anymore. Smoking is not allowed inside the theater.

One of our favorite places along Rustaveli Avenue was a lemonade parlor called Laghidze Waters. It had been a favorite place for generations of Tbilisi dwellers. Laghidze Waters had an interesting history, as the firm was founded at the end of the nineteenth century by a pharmacist, Mitrofane Laghidze. He meticulously selected and tested all of the fruit ingredients that created syrups for lemonades.

Inside the parlor, there were white granite countertops that held rows of soda fountains. There were big glass cones filled with a variety of syrups next to the fountains: pear, lemon, sour cherry, apple, chocolate, cream, and tarragon. You had to select your own flavor and order it. A sales assistant would pour the syrup in a tiny glass and mix it with the soda from the fountain in a larger glass and offer it to you. I was partial to lemon and tarragon. Laghidze Waters was one of the main attractions on Rustaveli Avenue. I was especially upset to see it gone now.

Just below Laghidze Waters was a restaurant specializing in *acharuli khachapuri*—traditional Georgian cheese bread from the Achara region, an open round or boat-shaped loaf with cheese stuffing and runny egg in the middle. It was a welcome nourishment after classes.

As the school was at the foot of Mount Mtatsminda, we sometimes climbed it. The slopes were beautiful in the spring, with cherry, almond, and apple trees blossoming in riots of colors. I knew shortcuts to Sololaki Mountain alleyways and the botanical garden there. One of the ugly manifestations of modern times is the unfortunate reality that general public access has been closed, as the whole mountain was acquired by an oligarch, a newcomer to Tbilisi who built a glass monstrosity on top of the mountain and thus changed the landscape of the city.

In my recollections, there is a solid presence symbolizing my childhood and serving as an anchor to moor me to my homeland. It is a tree. My school had a quadrangle and a beautiful sycamore tree in the middle. The tree was planted when St. Nino College was founded. The tree must be at least 172 years old today. It has seen many changes. After I had graduated, I learned that a part of the original school building was on the verge of collapse. They had to demolish the building and rebuild the entire school from scratch. The old school building is yet another vanished spot I had to commit to memory. But the tree survived.

Amidst the fading sites, the sycamore tree remains a faithful and loyal constant that carries over from my childhood. It still stands tall, strong, proud, and more mature than aged. We have all grown out of its shade and gone our separate ways, having left behind our sounds suspended in the tree branches to reemerge every spring with new promises and beginnings.

Ten

TASTES FROM MY CHILDHOOD

Mom's Easter Cake Recipe

Mom had several recipes for Easter cake. Most of them called for several dozen eggs and lots of milk and butter, as she shared her cakes with many friends and relatives. I chose the quickest and easiest one here.

Ingredients

1 liter milk
110–112 grams yeast powder
800 grams plus 2 cups flour, divided
700 grams plus 1 cup sugar, divided
500 grams butter
12 eggs, separated
3 tablespoons olive oil
6 tablespoons lemon essence
3 tablespoons vanilla extract
1 vanilla bean, scraped and very finely cut
4 teaspoons cardamom
4 teaspoons allspice
2 teaspoons nutmeg
1 teaspoon lemon zest
powdered sugar, for dusting

Procedure

1. Warm up milk on the stove to 80 degrees C.
2. Place yeast in a big enamel pot and pour warm milk over. Mix well by hand for 10 minutes, until the yeast is well dissolved.
3. Pour in 2 cups flour and 1 cup sugar. Mix again by hand until smooth and well dissolved.
4. Cover pot with a tea towel and leave for an hour in a warm place. For a quicker result, wrap the pot in a plastic bag or a thick cloth. Leave to rise 50–60 minutes in a warm kitchen.
5. Meanwhile, melt butter over low heat.
6. In a large bowl, combine egg whites and 500 grams sugar. Mix well on high speed until mixture is fluffy.
7. In a separate bowl, combine egg yolks and remaining 200 grams sugar. Mix on high speed for 15 minutes.
8. Add egg yolk mixture to egg white mixture. Add melted butter and mix again for 20 minutes.
9. When yeast mixture is ready, slowly add egg and butter mixture to enamel pot.
10. Add remaining 800 grams flour to the mixture through a sieve, gradually mixing it in with a wooden spoon. When all the flour is in, start mixing by hand again until smooth. Pour in olive oil.
11. In a small bowl, combine remaining ingredients except for powdered sugar. Sprinkle into dough. Do not stop mixing.
12. Dough is considered ready when it falls from the hand and does not stick. It should not be runny but should have the consistency of thick sour cream. Cover the pot and bundle it up in a warm blanket. Leave for 3 hours.
13. When dough is almost ready, preheat oven to 365 degrees F. Prepare tall molds. Wipe the insides lightly with olive oil or use nonstick spray.
14. After 3 hours, uncover pot. Drop dough into each mold, filling only halfway. Let filled molds sit another 10 minutes in the warm kitchen. Then put into preheated oven.

15. After 10 minutes, reduce heat by 20 degrees. Bake another 25 minutes. Do not open the oven to check on it. Check through the window in the oven door.

16. When dough has risen to the top of molds and browned up, switch off the oven. Do not take molds out immediately. Leave in oven another 10 minutes.

17. Remove molds from oven and then remove cakes from mold. Place on a tray.

18. When cakes have cooled off, dust tops with powdered sugar. Cover lightly and keep in a cool place until ready to serve.

Yield: One large, two medium, four small cakes

Mom's Sour Cream Cake

Ingredients

Dough:
200 grams sour cream
1 cup sugar
200 grams butter, softened
3 cups of flour
1 cup cocoa powder
Cream stuffing:
4 cups sour cream
1 cup sugar
1 cup walnuts chopped and lightly roasted
freshly squeezed juice from 2 lemons
Chocolate glaze:
1 cup sugar
4 tablespoons cocoa powder
4 tablespoons milk
50 grams butter

Procedure

Make the dough:

1. Preheat oven to 365 degrees F.
2. In a bowl, combine sour cream and sugar. Add butter. Mix well and add flour.
3. Divide dough into two equal parts. Mix cocoa powder well into one part.
4. Divide two parts further into two equal parts, making four pieces total.
5. Flatten pieces into thin sheets. Bake each piece separately in preheated oven, 10–12 minutes each or until a toothpick inserted in the center comes out clean.

Make the cream stuffing:

6. In a mixing bowl, combine all ingredients.
7. Spread cream over three of the baked cake sheets. Stack the cream-covered sheets, then put the fourth sheet on top.

Make the chocolate glaze:

8. In a saucepan, combine sugar, cocoa powder, and milk. Bring to boil.
9. Add butter. Reduce heat and leave until butter is well melted. Mix well and remove from stove.
10. Pour hot glaze over top of cake.

Yield: 16 servings

Grandma Sylvia's Beef Stroganoff

Ingredients

2 pounds sirloin steak
salt and pepper (to taste)
5 medium onions, thinly cut
3 tablespoons olive oil
1 tablespoon flour
1 cup sour cream
6 large potatoes, cut lengthwise into very thin slices and fried
chopped parsley, for garnish

Procedure

1. Cut pieces of steak into thin slices 2 centimeters wide and 5 centimeters lengthwise. Pound the pieces on both sides and put them in a pot. Season with salt and pepper. Put the pot into the refrigerator for an hour.
2. Remove pot from refrigerator and add onions. Add olive oil and sauté 20 minutes, mixing occasionally.
3. Add some water just to cover the meat. Bring to a boil and let simmer another 20 minutes.
4. In a glass, combine flour with 5 tablespoons cold water. Mix well to dissolve flour.
5. In a bowl, combine sour cream with flour mixture. Pour into pot and bring to a boil. Reduce heat and leave to simmer until meat becomes tender.
6. Put meat and sauce on a plate and serve potatoes on the side. Garnish with chopped parsley.

Yield: 8 – 12 servings

Mom's Eggplant Stuffed with Walnuts

I've updated this recipe just a little bit. If you have time, you can fry the eggplant slices instead of baking them, but that takes a lot of oil and more time, since you can't fry all the slices at once. Note that it is important to buy Italian eggplants, or even Chinese or Indian, but don't buy the large American eggplants. I have tried them. They come out mushy.

Ingredients

4 Italian eggplants
olive oil
1 full cup ground walnuts
small bunch cilantro, chopped
several leaves fresh basil, or 2 teaspoons dried
1 tablespoon vinegar
3/4 cup water
3–4 large garlic cloves, peeled
2 teaspoons coriander powder (I use coriander seeds and crush them together with garlic and salt)
1 teaspoon red pepper
salt (to taste)

1. Preheat oven to 375–380 degrees F.
2. Slice an unpeeled, well-washed eggplant lengthwise. You should get maybe 6 thin slices.
3. Spread slices on a baking sheet, sprinkle with olive oil, and bake for about 15 minutes, until golden brown, turning over halfway through. Check with a fork to see if the slices are tender; don't overcook. Remove from oven and let cool.
4. While eggplant is cooling off, prepare the stuffing: In a bowl, combine walnuts, some of the cilantro, basil, vinegar, and water. Add coriander powder or crushed coriander seeds. I prefer making my own powder. In a separate bowl, crush garlic cloves with

coriander seeds, red pepper, and salt. Add to walnut mixture and mix well.

5. Take a teaspoonful of stuffing and spread on one eggplant slice, like spreading butter on a piece of bread. Roll the slice up. Repeat with remaining slices and stuffing.

6. Place eggplant rolls on a dish, garnish with remaining cilantro and serve at room temperature.

Yield: 10 – 16 servings

My street. The house on the right is where I grew up.

In front of our house stands the tree that Dad saved.

My grandfather Benedicte (Beno) and grandmother Sylvia

Mom's family: (*sitting*) father Benedicte; mother Sylvia;
grandmother Martha; aunt Natela; uncle Giga; (*standing*)
brother Malkhaz; Mom; Giga's wife, Nunu; sister Lia

I love these old photos from the world that disappeared. My grandparents are young in this photo. It must be 1928 or 1929. My grandmother Sylvia is holding Mom. My great grandmother Martha is in the middle. Sitting in front is Giga, Sylvia's younger brother.

My great grandfather Giorgi Baramidze and his wife, Sonia
Imnadze, with some of their children. My grandfather
Benedicte is standing on the right. Vano, the little guy on
the extreme left, next to his dad, died from Spanish flu.

Dad's family: (*sitting*) father Bagrat; Dad; mother Nadya; sister Mariam, known to everyone as Tsutsa; (*standing*) uncle Levan. This must be the last family photo taken together.

Mom and Dad

When it started. Mom and Dad are at right in the second
row. Mom is a medical student; Dad is an assistant
professor in the department of general surgery.

Before and after World War II: Dad once told me that he liked this
photo taken before the war because he still had both legs in it.

In St. Petersburg: Mom, Dad, Gogi, and myself together with my uncle Malkhaz, who is standing on the left. We spent much time there with Dad when he worked on his doctoral dissertation at Pavlov Institute of Physiology.

All of us: Mom, Dad, Gogi, Revaz, and Nana

Dad at a lecture with medical school students

Gogi's birthday in Kvishkheti. Our grandparents visited
us, together with Lia and Iza. *Sitting*: Lia, Dad, Revaz, our
landlord's son, Gogi, Grandfather, myself, and Iza

Gogi and Nana at the Black Sea

Our family at different times in Bakuriani

Our neighbor from Tbilisi, Dad, Mom, and our
landlady between myself and Gogi

Mtskheta

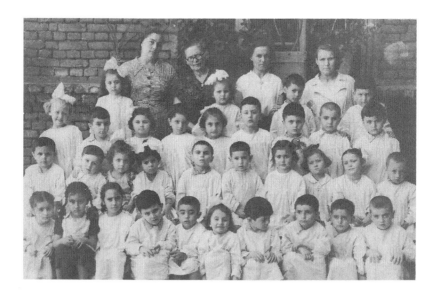

Kindergarten. We wore white coats on top of our clothes. I am
sitting in the second row, fourth from the right. Gogi is standing
behind me, second from the right. Even though we were in
different age groups, this photo has both of us together.

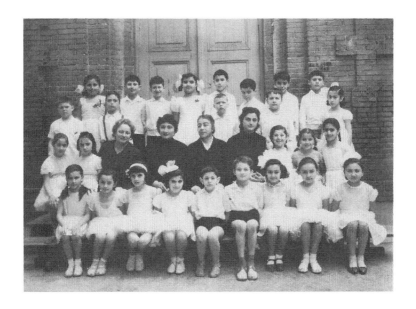

Second grade, the first year at the English school, after one of our
first performances. I am sitting in the second row, first on the left.

At one of our performances. I am the letter *L*
and recited a little poem on that letter.

In seventh grade. I am sitting in the second row, first right.

Pygmalion. I am Eliza Doolittle.

Mom and Dad in later years

The school sycamore tree

About the Author

Nana Khizanishvili grew up in Tbilisi, Georgia. She studied in Tbilisi and Moscow and holds a doctoral degree in comparative linguistics from Moscow State University. She was a professor of English at Tbilisi State University until she relocated to the United States together with her family in 1992 and was a visiting professor at Meredith College in North Carolina. She developed the Georgian language course and taught Georgian to State Department employees for several years. Currently, she is a software quality analyst. Her daughters, Tika and Annie, grew up in the United States. Nana has three grandchildren. She lives in a suburb of Washington, DC, with her husband and her yellow lab, Gabo.

Made in the USA
Middletown, DE
04 November 2019